Contents

2

Chocolate-dipped Meringue Sandwich Cookies

Serving: 7 dozen. | Prep: 60m | Ready in: 01h40m

Ingredients

- 4 large egg whites
- 1 cup confectioners' sugar
- 1/2 cup almond flour
- 2/3 cup sugar
- GANACHE:
- 6 oz. semisweet chocolate, chopped
- 3 oz. unsweetened chocolate, chopped
- 1-1/4 cups heavy whipping cream
- 1 tbsp. light corn syrup
- TOPPINGS:
- 1/2 cup chocolate sprinkles
- 1/2 cup sliced almonds, finely chopped and toasted
- 1/2 cup sweetened shredded coconut, finely chopped and toasted

Direction

1. In a big bowl, put egg whites then let rest for 30 minutes at room temperature.
2. Heat the oven beforehand to 225 degrees. Whisk almond flour and confectioners' sugar until mixed in a small bowl. Mix egg whites until foamy on medium speed. Put sugar in gradually, one tbsp. at a time. Mix on high before putting the next until sugar dissolves. Keep on beating until get stiff flossy peaks formed then fold in the confectioners' sugar mixture.
3. Cut a small hole in the corner of a food-safe plastic bag or in the tip of a pastry bag. Insert #805 round pastry tip then put meringue to fill the bag. Pipe 1-inch diameter cookies on baking sheets lined with parchment paper, leaving 1-inch space apart each cookies. Make the tops of the cookies smooth by using a finger moistened with water.
4. Bake until it becomes firm to the touch or for 40 to 45 minutes. Turn the oven off but do not open its door. Let the cookies rest for an hour in oven. Take out from the oven and allow to completely cool on the baking sheets.
5. Make the ganache by putting unsweetened and semisweet chocolates in a small bowl. Mix corn syrup and cream in a small saucepan then bring just to a boil. Pour on the chocolate then mix until it becomes smooth using a whisk. Put a cup of ganache to a different bowl then put in the refrigerator and occasionally stir until mixture is thick enough to pipe, or for 25 to 30 minutes. Set aside the rest of the ganache for dipping. Let rest with a cover, occasionally stirring, at room temperature.
6. Cut a small hole in a corner of a food-safe plastic bag or in the tip of a pastry bag. Insert #802 round pastry tip then put ganache in to fill the bag. Pipe the ganache onto the half of the cookies' bottoms. Use the remaining cookies to cover. As the ganache warms, it may become soft. Put back in the refrigerator until it becomes firm enough to pipe, if necessary. In different shallow bowls, transfer the toppings. Immerse every sandwich cookie halfway in room temperature ganache. Let excess drip off. Dunk the

toppings in as you prefer. Put on waxed paper and let rest until set; keep at room temperature in an airtight container.

Chocolate-dipped Strawberry Meringue Roses

Serving: *2 dozen. | Prep: 25m | Ready in: 01h05m*

Ingredients

- 3 large egg whites
- 1/4 cup sugar
- 1/4 cup freeze-dried strawberries
- 1 package (3 oz.) strawberry gelatin
- 1/2 tsp. vanilla extract, optional
- 1 cup 60% cacao bittersweet chocolate baking chips, melted

Direction

1. Put egg whites in big bowl; stand for 30 minutes at room temperature. Preheat an oven to 225°.
2. Process strawberries and sugar till powdery in food processor. Put gelatin in; pulse to blend.
3. On medium speed, beat egg whites till foamy; if desired, add vanilla. 1 tbsp. at a time, add gelatin mixture slowly, beating on high after every addition till sugar melts. Beat till stiff glossy peaks form.
4. Cut small hole in corner of food-safe plastic bag/ in tip of pastry bag; insert #1M star tip. Put meringue in bag; pipe 2-in. roses on parchment paper-lined baking sheets, 1 1/2-in. apart.
5. Bake till dry and set, 40-45 minutes. Turn oven off without opening oven door. Lcave meringues for 1 1/2 hours in oven. Take out of oven; on baking sheets, completely cool.
6. Take meringues from paper; in melted chocolate, dip bottoms. Let excess drip off. Put on waxed paper; stand for 45 minutes till set. Keep at room temperature in airtight container.

Nutrition Information: Calories: 33 calories Total Carbohydrate: 6 g Cholesterol: 0 mg Total Fat: 1 g Fiber: 0 g Protein: 1 g Sodium: 9 mg

Chocolate-raspberry Cutout Cookies

Serving: *4 dozen. | Prep: 45m | Ready in: 55m*

Ingredients

- 1 cup unsalted butter, softened
- 1 cup superfine sugar
- 1 large egg
- 1 large egg yolk
- 2 tsps. vanilla extract
- 2-1/4 cups all-purpose flour
- 1/4 cup baking cocoa
- 1/2 tsp. salt

- 1/4 tsp. baking powder
- 1/4 tsp. ground cinnamon
- FROSTING:
- 1-1/2 cups frozen unsweetened raspberries, thawed
- 6 tbsps. butter, softened
- 4 cups confectioners' sugar
- Gold and pearl dragees

Direction

1. Cream sugar and butter till fluffy and light in big bowl; beat vanilla, yolk and egg in. Mix cinnamon, baking powder, cocoa, salt and flour; add to creamed mixture slowly. Stir well.
2. Halve dough; form each portion into ball. Flatten into disk; use plastic to wrap. Refrigerate for an hour.
3. Roll one dough portion to 1/4-in. thick on lightly floured surface; use floured 3-in. heart-shaped cookie cutter to cut. Put on greased baking sheets, 1-in. apart. Repeat with leftover dough.
4. Bake for 6-8 minutes at 375° till lightly browned; cool for a minute. Transfer from pans onto wire racks; completely cool.
5. Frosting: Through sieve, press raspberries; discard seeds. Cream raspberry puree, confectioners' sugar and butter till creamy and smooth in big bowl. Frost and decorate cookies with dragees as desired. Keep in airtight container in the fridge.

Nutrition Information: Calories: 128 calories Total Carbohydrate: 19 g Cholesterol: 22 mg Total Fat: 6 g Fiber: 0 g Protein: 1 g Sodium: 39 mg

Chocolate-raspberry Whoopie Pies

Serving: about 2-1/2 dozen. | Prep: 40m | Ready in: 50m

Ingredients

- 1/2 cup butter, softened
- 1 cup sugar
- 1 large egg
- 1 tsp. vanilla extract
- 2 cups all-purpose flour
- 1/2 cup baking cocoa
- 1-1/2 tsps. baking soda
- 1/2 tsp. baking powder
- 1/2 tsp. salt
- 1 cup 2% milk
- FILLING:
- 1 jar (7 oz.) marshmallow creme
- 1/2 cup shortening
- 1/3 cup seedless raspberry jam
- 1 tsp. vanilla extract
- 2 cups confectioners' sugar

Direction

1. Preheat an oven to 400°. Cream sugar and butter till fluffy and light in big bowl. Beat vanilla and egg in. Whisk salt, baking powder, baking soda, cocoa and flour in separate bowl; alternately with milk, add to creamed mixture, beating well with every addition.
2. By tablespoonfuls, drop dough on greased baking sheets, 2-in. apart. Bake for 6-8 minutes till set and lightly touched tops spring back. Transfer from pans onto wire racks; completely cool.
3. Filling: Beat shortening and marshmallow crème till blended in big bowl. Beat vanilla and jam in; beat confectioners' sugar in slowly till smooth. On bottoms of 1/2 of cookies, spread; use leftover cookies to cover.

Nutrition Information: Calories: 186 calories Total Carbohydrate: 30 g Cholesterol: 15 mg Total Fat: 7 g Fiber: 0 g Protein: 2 g Sodium: 148 mg

Classic Crisp Sugar Cookies

Serving: 6 dozen. | Prep: 15m | Ready in: 25m

Ingredients

• 1-1/2 cups Domino® or C&H® Pure Cane Granulated Sugar
• 1/2 cup butter, softened
• 1/2 cup shortening
• 2 eggs
• 3 tbsps. sour cream
• 1 tsp. vanilla extract
• 3 cups all-purpose flour
• 1/2 tsp. baking soda
• 1/2 tsp. salt
• Domino® or C&H® Pure Cane Powdered Sugar
• Additional Domino® or C&H® Pure Cane Granulated Sugar

Direction

1. Cream shortening, butter and sugar till fluffy and light in big bowl; one by one, add eggs. Beat vanilla and sour cream in. Mix salt, baking soda and flour; add to creamed mixture slowly. Stir well. Cover; refrigerate till dough becomes easy to handle, about a minimum of 30 minutes.
2. Roll dough out to 1/8-in. thick on powdered sugar-covered surface. Use floured 2 1/2-in. cookie cutters to cut; put on ungreased baking sheets, 1-in. apart. Sprinkle granulated sugar over; bake for 7-8 minutes at 350° till edges lightly brown. Transfer to wire racks; cool.

Espresso Shortbread Squares

Serving: 25 cookies. | Prep: 15m | Ready in: 35m

Ingredients

• 1 tbsp. instant espresso powder

- 1 tbsp. hot water
- 1 cup butter, softened
- 2/3 cup confectioners' sugar
- 1/2 tsp. vanilla extract
- 2 cups all-purpose flour
- 1 cup white baking chips
- 1/2 cup dried cherries, coarsely chopped
- Additional confectioners' sugar

Direction

1. Melt espresso powder in hot water in small bowl. Cream confectioners' sugar and butter till fluffy and light in big bowl; beat melted espresso mixture and vanilla in. Beat flour in slowly. Mix cherries and baking chips in.
2. Pat dough to 10-in. square on plastic wrap sheet; tightly wrap. Refrigerate for a minimum of 2 hours till firm.
3. Preheat an oven to 325° then unwrap dough. Cut to 2-in. squares. Put on parchment paper-lined baking sheet, 1-in. apart. Use fork to prick holes in every cookie; bake till set, 20-25 minutes.
4. Transfer from pans onto wire racks; completely cool. Lightly dust with extra confectioners' sugar; keep in airtight containers.

Fancy Sugar Cookies

Serving: about 1-1/2 dozen. | Prep: 30m | Ready in: 38m

Ingredients

- 1-1/2 cups Domino® or C&H® Pure Cane Granulated Sugar
- 1 cup butter-flavored shortening
- 2 eggs
- 3 tbsps. sour cream
- 1 tsp. vanilla extract
- 1/2 tsp. lemon extract
- 3 cups all-purpose flour
- 1/2 tsp. baking soda
- 1/2 tsp. salt
- Domino® or C&H® Pure Cane Powdered Sugar
- COLORED SUGAR CRYSTALS:
- 2 tbsps. Domino® or C&H® Pure Cane Granulated Sugar
- 1 to 2 drops food coloring

Direction

1. Cream the sugar and shortening until fluffy and light in a big bowl. Put eggs in, 1 at a time. Stir well before putting the next. Beat in lemon extract, vanilla and sour cream. Mix salt, baking soda and flour then put in the creamed mixture. Stir well. Cover and put in the refrigerator until easy to handle or for a

minimum of 30 minutes.

2. Roll out 1/2 of the dough into 1/8-inch thickness on a surface covered with powder sugar. Cut using 2 1/2-inch floured cookie cutters. Put on cookie sheets with grease, leaving 1 inch space apart. Roll the rest of the dough out to 1/8 inch thickness then slice into lattice-style strips. Criss-cross the strips in lattice style on top of the cutout cookies, pressing its ends lightly to the cookies. Trim the strips if needed. Collect the scraps then roll and cut them again.

3. To make the colored sugar crystals, mix food coloring and sugar using the back of a spoon to blend. Sprinkle over the cookies with lattice on top. Bake until it turns lightly browned or for 7 to 8 minutes at 350 degrees. Transfer to wire racks; cool.

Festive Chocolate Hearts

Serving: about 4 dozen. | Prep: 30m | Ready in: 40m

Ingredients

- 1 cup butter, cubed
- 2/3 cup packed brown sugar
- 1 tsp. vanilla extract
- 1 egg, lightly beaten
- 2-1/4 cups all-purpose flour
- 1/4 cup baking cocoa
- 1/2 tsp. salt
- 3/4 cup finely chopped walnuts
- TOPPING:
- 1-1/2 cups scmisweet chocolate chips
- 2 tbsps. shortening
- Red nonpareils

Direction

1. Mix and cook brown sugar and butter in saucepan on medium-low heat till butter melts. Take off heat; mix vanilla in. Cool for 15 minutes; mix egg in.

2. Mix salt, cocoa and flour; add to butter mixture. Fold walnuts in. Cover; chill till easy to handle, about 30 minutes.

3. Roll dough to 1/4-in. thick on lightly floured surface. Use floured 3-in. heart-shaped cookie cutter to cut; put on ungreased baking sheets, 1-in. apart. Bake for 9-10 minutes till edges are firm at 350°. Transfer onto wire racks; cool.

4. Topping: Melt shortening and chocolate chips in microwave on low heat; mix till smooth. Slightly cool. Spread thin chocolate mixture layer with small spatula around cookies' edges; sprinkle nonpareils over. Put on waxed paper; stand till set.

For-my-love Sugar Cookies

Serving: about 5-1/2 dozen. | Prep: 20m | Ready in: 30m

Ingredients

- 3/4 cup shortening
- 1-1/2 cups sugar
- 2 eggs
- 3 cups self-rising flour
- 1 tsp. orange extract
- Colored sugar, optional

Direction

1. Cream sugar and shortening till fluffy and light in big bowl; beat extract and eggs in. Add flour slowly; stir well. Cover; refrigerate till easy to handle, 1 hour.
2. Roll dough out to 1/4-in. thick on floured surface; use lightly floured 2-in. cookie cutters to cut. If desired, sprinkle colored sugar over.
3. Put on ungreased baking sheets, 1-in. apart. Bake for 6-8 minutes till lightly browned at 375°; transfer to wire racks then cool.

Nutrition Information: Calories: 117 calories Total Carbohydrate: 17 g Cholesterol: 13 mg Total Fat: 5 g Fiber: 0 g Protein: 1 g Sodium: 135 mg

Frosted Cherry Chip Cookies

Serving: 3-1/2 dozen. | Prep: 60m | Ready in: 01h15m

Ingredients

- 1 jar (10 oz.) maraschino cherries
- 6 tbsps. butter, softened
- 1 cup sugar
- 1 egg
- 1 tsp. vanilla extract
- 2 cups all-purpose flour
- 1/2 tsp. baking soda
- 1/2 tsp. salt
- 1/2 cup sour cream
- FROSTING:
- 3-1/2 cups confectioners' sugar
- 1/2 cup sour cream
- Red colored sugar, optional

Direction

1. Let the cherries drain and save 1 tbsp. of juice for frosting. Slice the cherries and pat dry; put aside. Cream the sugar and butter in a big bowl. Stir in vanilla and egg. Mix salt, baking soda and flour then put alternately with the sour cream into the creamed mixture. Mix in the cherries.
2. Drop by tablespoonfuls on baking sheets with grease, leaving 2-inchspaces apart. Bake until lightly

browned or for 12 to 15 minutes at 350 degrees. Allow to cool by moving to wire racks.

3. For the frosting, combine the reserved cherry juice, sour cream and confectioners' sugar until smooth in a bowl. Pour mixture over cookies and if desired, use colored sugar to sprinkle on top.

Nutrition Information: Calories: 115 calories Total Carbohydrate: 22 g Cholesterol: 13 mg Total Fat: 3 g Fiber: 0 g Protein: 1 g Sodium: 64 mg

Frosted Chocolate Cherry Cookies

Serving: about 2-1/2 dozen. | Prep: 20m | Ready in: 30m

Ingredients

• 1/2 cup butter, softened
• 1 cup sugar
• 1 egg
• 1-1/2 tsps. vanilla extract
• 1-1/2 cups all-purpose flour
• 1/2 cup baking cocoa
• 1/2 tsp. salt, divided
• 1/4 tsp. baking powder
• 1/4 tsp. baking soda
• 1 jar (10 oz.) maraschino cherries
• 1 cup (6 oz.) semisweet chocolate chips
• 1/2 cup sweetened condensed milk

Direction

1. Cream sugar and butter in bowl. Add vanilla and egg; stir well. Mix baking soda, baking powder, 1/4 tsp. salt, cocoa and flour; add to creamed mixture slowly.
2. Drain cherries; keep 1 1/2 tsp. juice. Pat dry cherries; form 1 tbsp. dough around every cherry. Put on ungreased baking sheets, 2-in. apart. Bake for 8-10 minutes till set at 350°. On wire racks, cool.
3. Frosting: Heat milk and chocolate chips till chips melt in saucepan; mix till smooth. Take off heat; add leftover salt and reserved cherry juice. Frost cookies.

Nutrition Information: Calories: 275 calories Total Carbohydrate: 44 g Cholesterol: 34 mg Total Fat: 11 g Fiber: 2 g Protein: 4 g Sodium: 187 mg

Mint Candy Cookies

Serving: about 3-1/2 dozen. | Prep: 20m | Ready in: 30m

Ingredients

• 1 package (17-1/2 oz.) sugar cookie mix
• 40 to 45 mint Andes candies
• 6 oz. pink candy coating disks
• Heart-shaped decorating sprinkles, optional

Direction

1. Make the cookie dough according to the directions in the package. Cover and let chill until it becomes easy to handle or for 15 to 20 minutes.
2. Pat a scant tablespoonful of dough in a thin layer, encircling each mint candy. Put on baking sheets without grease, leaving 2-inch space apart. Bake until set or for 7 to 9 minutes at 375 degrees. Let to cool for 1 minutes then allow to cool completely by transferring wire racks from pans.
3. Melt candy coating in a microwave-safe bowl then mix until it becomes smooth. Drizzle on top of cookies. If desired, put decorating sprinkles on top.

Mint Chocolate Wafers

Serving: 10 dozen. | Prep: 60m | Ready in: 01h10m

Ingredients

- 1 large egg
- 1/3 cup water
- 3 tbsps. canola oil
- 1 package chocolate fudge cake mix (regular size)
- 1/2 cup cake flour
- COATING:
- 4 cups (24 oz.) semisweet chocolate chips
- 1/4 cup shortening
- 1/2 tsp. peppermint extract
- Sprinkles

Direction

1. Beat oil, water and egg until mixed in a big bowl. Beat in flour and cake mix gradually.
2. Halve the dough. Form each into a disk then wrap with plastic. Put in the refrigerator until it becomes firm enough to roll or for 2 hours.
3. Heat the oven beforehand to 350 degrees. Roll each portion of the dough, making 1/8-inch thickness on a lightly floured surface. Cut the dough using a 1 1/2-inch floured round cookie cutter. Put on baking sheets with grease, leaving 1 inch space apart.
4. Bake it until it becomes firm or for 8 to 10 minutes. Allow to completely cool by transferring to wire racks from pans.
5. Melt shortening and chocolate chips in top of a double broiler or a metal bowl over hot water. Mix until it becomes smooth. Mix extract in. Spread chocolate mixture on the cookies. Put on baking sheets lined with waxed paper then use sprinkles to decorate. Keep in the refrigerator until set.

Mocha Cherry Cookies

Serving: about 3 dozen. | Prep: 20m | Ready in: 40m

Ingredients

- 1 cup butter, softened
- 1/2 cup sugar
- 1 tsp. vanilla extract
- 1 tsp. instant coffee granules
- 1 tsp. hot water
- 1/4 cup baking cocoa
- 2 cups all-purpose flour
- 1/2 cup chopped maraschino cherries
- 1/2 cup chopped walnuts
- Additional sugar
- Melted semisweet chocolate, optional

Direction

1. Cream the sugar and butter and fluffy in a bowl. Put in vanilla. Dissolve the coffee granules in water then put in the creamed mixture with cocoa. Put the flour then stir well. Mix in walnuts and cherries. Form 1 1/4-inch balls then roll in the sugar. Put on baking sheets without grease. Bake for 20 to 22 minutes at 325 degrees. Allow to cool by putting on wire racks. If desired, drizzle chocolate.

Nutrition Information: Calories: 196 calories Total Carbohydrate: 20 g Cholesterol: 27 mg Total Fat: 12 g Fiber: 1 g Protein: 3 g Sodium: 106 mg

Mocha Macaroon Cookies

Serving: about 4 dozen. | Prep: 20m | Ready in: 30m

Ingredients

- 2 tsps. instant coffee granules
- 2 tsps. hot water
- 1 can (14 oz.) sweetened condensed milk
- 2 oz. unsweetened chocolate, melted
- 1 tsp. vanilla extract
- 1/4 tsp. ground cinnamon
- 1/8 tsp. salt
- 1 package (14 oz.) sweetened shredded coconut
- 2/3 cup white baking chips, melted
- Plain or chocolate-covered coffee beans, optional

Direction

1. Heat the oven beforehand to 350 degrees. Dissolve coffee granules in a big bowl with hot water. Mix in salt, cinnamon, vanilla, melted chocolate and condensed milk until blended. Mix in coconut; by rounded teaspoonfuls, drop the mixture on baking sheets lined with parchment paper, leaving 2 inches space apart.
2. Bake it until set or for 10 to 12 minutes. Allow it to cool on the pans for a minute; let to cool completely by putting on wire racks.

3. Drizzle melted baking chips over cookies then put coffee beans on top – if necessary, attach with the melted chips.

Nutrition Information: Calories: 87 calories Total Carbohydrate: 10 g Cholesterol: 3 mg Total Fat: 5 g Fiber: 1 g Protein: 1 g Sodium: 41 mg

Mocha Pecan Balls

Serving: *Makes about 95 cookies*

Ingredients

- 2 sticks (1 cup) unsalted butter, softened
- 1/2 cup granulated sugar
- 2 tsps. vanilla
- 1 tbsp. instant espresso powder
- 1/4 cup unsweetened cocoa powder
- 3/4 tsp. salt
- 1 3/4 cups all-purpose flour
- 2 cups finely chopped pecans
- confectioners' sugar for coating the cookies

Direction

1. Use electric mixer to cream granulated sugar and butter till fluffy and light in a bowl. Add salt, cocoa powder, espresso powder and vanilla; beat till well combined. Add flour; beat till dough just combines. Beat pecans in. Chill dough for a minimum of 2 hours up to overnight, covered.
2. Preheat an oven to 375°F; roll dough to 1-in. balls. Put on baking sheets, 1-in. apart. In batches, bake cookies in center of oven till just firm, about 12-15 minutes; cool on sheets for 5 minutes. In batches, toss warm cookies in bowl of confectioners' sugar till well coated. You can make cookies 2 months ahead, and keep in airtight containers, frozen.

Nutrition Information: Calories: 47 Total Carbohydrate: 3 g Cholesterol: 5 mg Total Fat: 4 g Fiber: 0 g Protein: 1 g Sodium: 19 mg
- Saturated Fat: 1 g

Mole New Mexican Wedding Cookies

Serving: *2-1/2 dozen. | Prep: 30m | Ready in: 45m*

Ingredients

- 1/2 cup butter, softened
- 3/4 cup confectioners' sugar, divided
- 1 tsp. vanilla extract
- 1 cup all-purpose flour
- 1/2 cup ground pecans
- 1 tsp. chili powder

- 1/4 tsp. ground cinnamon
- 1/4 tsp. ground cloves
- 1/4 tsp. ground allspice
- 1/2 cup miniature semisweet chocolate chips

Direction

1. Heat the oven beforehand to 350 degrees. Cream the 1/3 cup of confectioners' sugar and butter until fluffy and light, then stir in vanilla. Whisk the next 6 ingredients together in a different bowl; mix in the creamed mixture gradually. Fold the chocolate chips in.
2. Form dough into 1-inch balls then put on baking sheets without grease, leaving 1-inch space apart. Bake for 12 to 15 minutes until the bottoms turn light brown. Allow to cool for 5 minutes by transferring to wire racks from pans. Roll in the leftover confectioners' sugar; cool completely.

Nutrition Information: Calories: 81 calories Total Carbohydrate: 8 g Cholesterol: 8 mg Total Fat: 5 g Fiber: 1 g Protein: 1 g Sodium: 27 mg

Mom's Soft Sugar Cookies

Serving: about 7-1/2 dozen. | Prep: 20m | Ready in: 30m

Ingredients

- 4 cups all-purpose flour
- 1 tsp. baking powder
- 1/2 tsp. nutmeg
- 1 cup butter, softened
- 1-3/4 cups sugar
- 3/4 tsp. salt
- 4 large egg yolks
- 2 large eggs
- 1 tsp. baking soda
- 2 tbsps. hot water
- 1 cup sour cream
- Optional toppings: colored or granulated sugar and walnut halves

Direction

1. Whisk nutmeg, baking powder and flour in a big bowl. Cream the salt, sugar and butter in a different bowl till fluffy and light. Stir in eggs, and egg yolks. Use hot water to dissolve baking soda, then put in the creamed mixture together with the sour cream. Stir in flour mixture gradually. The dough will seem sticky. Put in the refrigerator with cover; leave overnight.
2. Heat the oven beforehand to 350 degrees. Do with 1/3 of batch at a time. Roll the dough into 1/4-inch thickness on a surface that is well-floured. Cover and put the leftover dough in the refrigerator until ready to roll. Slice using 2 1/2-inch round cookie cutter or other shaped one. Put on baking sheets with grease, leaving 1 inch space apart. Sprinkle using sugar and put walnuts on top if preferred.
3. Bake until cookies are set but not browned or for 8 to 10 minutes. Allow to cool by transferring to wire

racks from pans.

Nutrition Information: Calories: 63 calories Total Carbohydrate: 8 g Cholesterol: 18 mg Total Fat: 3 g Fiber: 0 g Protein: 1 g Sodium: 58 mg

No-bake Cookie Balls

Serving: about 5 dozen. | Prep: 25m | Ready in: 25m

Ingredients

- 1 cup (6 oz.) semisweet chocolate chips
- 3 cups confectioners' sugar
- 1-3/4 cups crushed vanilla wafers (about 55 wafers)
- 1 cup chopped walnuts, toasted
- 1/3 cup orange juice
- 3 tbsps. light corn syrup
- Additional confectioners' sugar

Direction

1. Melt the chocolate chips in a microwave then mix until it becomes smooth. Mix in corn syrup, orange juice, walnuts, vanilla wafers and confectioners' sugar.
2. Form into 1-inch balls then roll in the additional confectioners' sugar. Keep in an airtight container.

Nutrition Information: Calories: 69 calories Total Carbohydrate: 12 g Cholesterol: 1 mg Total Fat: 3 g Fiber: 0 g Protein: 1 g Sodium: 12 mg

Nuts-about-you Cookie Sticks

Serving: about 2-1/2 dozen. | Prep: 5m | Ready in: 10m

Ingredients

- 1 cup semisweet chocolate chips
- 1 tbsp. shortening
- 2 tbsps. creamy peanut butter
- 1 can (13-1/2 oz.) Pirouette cookies
- 1/2 cup chopped nuts

Direction

1. Melt the peanut butter, shortening and chocolate chips in a microwave. Mix until it becomes smooth. Dunk 1 end of each cookie in the chocolate mixture and let the excess drip off. Sprinkle using nuts and put it on waxed paper. Let rest until set.

Nutrition Information: Calories: 111 calories Total Carbohydrate: 13 g Cholesterol: 5 mg Total Fat: 7 g Fiber: 1 g Protein: 1 g Sodium: 34 mg

Oatmeal Valentine Cookies

Serving: 2-1/2 dozen 3-inch cookies. | Prep: 15m | Ready in: 30m

Ingredients

- 2-1/2 cups all-purpose flour
- 1 tsp. baking powder
- 1/2 tsp. salt
- 3/4 cup butter, softened
- 3/4 cup sugar
- 1 large egg
- 2 tbsps. whole milk
- 1 tsp. vanilla extract
- 1 cup old-fashioned oats
- Red colored sugar, optional

Direction

1. Whisk the salt, flour and baking powder together. Cream the sugar and butter for about 5 minutes until fluffy and light in a big bowl. Put the milk, vanilla and egg then beat together until it becomes smooth. Mix the oats in.
2. Make 1/8-inchess thick dough by rolling it on a surface with flour. Slice the dough into heart shapes then put it on baking sheets without grease. If desired, use red sugar to decorate the dough. Bake it until it turns light golden brown or for 15 to 18mins at 375 degrees. Allow it to cool completely by transferring it to wire racks.

Nutrition Information: Calories: 221 calories Total Carbohydrate: 30 g Cholesterol: 39 mg Total Fat: 10 g Fiber: 1 g Protein: 4 g Sodium: 204 mg

Raspberry Kisses

Serving: Makes 2 doz. or 12 servings, 2 cookie sandwiches each. | Prep: 10m | Ready in: 10m

Ingredients

- 48 vanilla wafers
- 1/2 cup (1/2 of 8-oz. tub) PHILADELPHIA Cream Cheese Spread
- 1/4 cup seedless raspberry jam or preserves
- 1 Tbsp. powdered sugar

Direction

1. Pour 1 tsp. of cream cheese spread on every piece or 24 wafers. Put half tsp. of jam on top.
2. Cover using the rest of the wafers to make sandwiches.
3. Sprinkle over using sugar.

Nutrition Information: Calories: 120 Total Carbohydrate: 16 g Cholesterol: 15 mg Total Fat: 6 g Fiber: 0 g

Protein: 1 g Sodium: 105 mg
- Sugar: 11 g
- Saturated Fat: 5 g

Raspberry Linzer Cookies

Serving: 32 | Prep: 20m | Ready in: 2h

Ingredients

- 2 cups all-purpose flour
- 1/2 tsp. baking soda
- 1/4 tsp. salt
- 1/4 tsp. ground cinnamon
- 3/4 cup white sugar
- 1/2 cup butter at room temperature
- 1/4 cup egg substitute
- 1 tsp. vanilla extract
- 1/4 cup seedless raspberry jam
- 1 tbsp. confectioners' sugar, or as needed

Direction

1. In a bowl, combine cinnamon, salt, flour and baking soda using a whisk.
2. Mix butter and white sugar in a bowl using an electric mixer on high until it becomes fluffy and light. Put vanilla extract and egg substitute; stir until blended well.
3. Mix flour mixture gradually into sugar-butter mixture until the dough becomes soft. Cut the dough into two equal balls. Use plastic wrap to wrap each ball. Put the dough in the refrigerator for a minimum of one hour.
4. Heat the oven beforehand to 190°C or 375°F. Put parchment papers into 2 baking sheets.
5. Make 1/8-inch thick rectangle by rolling the dough on a lightly floured surface with. Make 32 cookies by cutting the dough using circular, star or square cookie cutter. Do it again with the second ball of dough. Use 1-inch square cookie cutter to cut the middle of 32 cookies. Put the 64 cookies on the baking sheets that were prepared, leaving about 1-inch space apart.
6. Bake the cookies for about 10 minutes, until the edges are lightly browned in the preheated oven. Let cool on pans for 5 minutes then allow to cool by putting on wire racks.
7. In the middle of each whole cookie, spread about half tsp. of raspberry jam. Use confectioners' sugar to sprinkle on the cut-out cookies. Put once piece of cut-out cookie over the cookie with raspberry jam on top.

Nutrition Information: Calories: 82 calories; Total Carbohydrate: 6 g Cholesterol: 8 mg Total Fat: 3 g Protein: 1 g Sodium: 62 mg

Raspberry Pistachio Thumbprints

Serving: about 3 dozen. | Prep: 25m | Ready in: 40m

Ingredients

- 1 cup butter, softened
- 1/2 cup confectioners' sugar
- 1 tsp. vanilla extract
- 2 cups all-purpose flour
- 1/4 tsp. salt
- 1 cup finely chopped pistachios
- 1/2 cup seedless raspberry jam
- Additional confectioners' sugar, optional

Direction

1. Preheat an oven to 325°; cream confectioners' sugar and butter till fluffy and light. Beat vanilla in. Whisk salt and flour in another bowl; beat into creamed mixture slowly. Add pistachios; stir well.
2. Form dough to 1-in. balls; put on ungreased baking sheets, 1-in. apart. Press deep indentation in middle of each using your thumb then fill each using 1/2 tsp. jam.
3. Bake for 13-16 minutes till bottoms are light brown. Transfer from pans onto wire racks; cool. Dust with extra confectioners' sugar if desired.

Nutrition Information: Calories: 97 calories Total Carbohydrate: 10 g Cholesterol: 12 mg Total Fat: 6 g Fiber: 0 g Protein: 1 g Sodium: 65 mg

Raspberry Sandwich Cookies

Serving: *about 2 dozen. | Prep: 01h30m | Ready in: 01h45m*

Ingredients

- 3 cups all-purpose flour
- 3/4 cup sugar
- 1/4 tsp. salt
- 1-1/2 cups cold butter
- 2 tbsps. cold water
- 1/2 tsp. almond extract
- 1/2 tsp. vanilla extract
- 3/4 cup seedless raspberry jam
- Confectioners' sugar

Direction

1. Mix salt, sugar and flour in big bowl; cut butter in till it looks like coarse crumbs. Mix extracts and water in till mixture becomes a ball.
2. Roll dough out to 1/8-in. thick on lightly floured surface; use floured 2 1/2-in. cookie cutters to cut. Cut out 1 1/2-in. shape from middle of 1/2 cookies; put on parchment paper-lined baking sheets, 1-in. apart.
3. Bake for 12-15 minutes at 325° till edges lightly brown; cool for 2 minutes. Transfer onto wire racks; completely cool.

4. Spread 1/2 tsp. jam on bottoms of solid cookies; sprinkle confectioners' sugar on cutout cookies. Put over the cookies with jam.

Nutrition Information: Calories: 207 calories Total Carbohydrate: 25 g Cholesterol: 30 mg Total Fat: 12 g Fiber: 0 g Protein: 2 g Sodium: 106 mg

Raspberry Snowflake Sandwich Cookies

Serving: about 1-1/2 dozen. | Prep: 20m | Ready in: 30m

Ingredients

- 1/2 cup butter, softened
- 1/4 cup shortening
- 3/4 cup sugar
- 1 large egg
- 1 tbsp. lemon juice
- 2 cups all-purpose flour
- 1-1/2 tsps. baking powder
- 1/2 tsp. ground cinnamon
- 1/4 tsp. salt
- 1/4 tsp. ground nutmeg
- 2 drinking straws (different sizes)
- 1/2 cup seedless raspberry jam
- Confectioners' sugar

Direction

1. Cream sugar, shortening and butter till fluffy and light in big bowl; beat lemon juice and egg in. Whisk nutmeg, salt, cinnamon, baking powder and flour in separate bowl; beat into creamed mixture slowly.
2. Halve dough; form each into a disk. Use plastic to wrap; refrigerate till firm enough to roll, 2 hours.
3. Preheat an oven to 375°; roll each dough portion to 1/8-in. thick on well-floured surface. Use floured 2 1/2-in. scalloped round cookie cutter to cut; cut several holes in 1/2 of the cutouts with straws. Twist straws to release. Put cutouts on baking sheets, 2-in. apart.
4. Bake till edges are light brown, about 6-8 minutes; slightly cool on pan. Transfer from pans onto wire racks; completely cool.
5. Spread 1 tsp. jam over bottoms of the solid cookies; use cutout cookies to top. Sprinkle confectioners' sugar over cookies.

Raspberry-almond Crescent Cookies

Serving: 4 dozen. | Prep: 45m | Ready in: 60m

Ingredients

- 2 cups all-purpose flour
- 1 cup cold butter, cubed

- 1 large egg yolk
- 1/2 cup sour cream
- 1 tsp. vanilla extract
- FILLING:
- 1 cup seedless raspberry jam
- 3/4 cup sweetened shredded coconut
- 1/3 cup finely chopped almonds
- 1/4 tsp. almond extract
- 1 large egg white, lightly beaten
- Coarse sugar

Direction

1. Put flour in a big bowl. Slice butter in the mixture until it looks like coarse crumbs. Whisk vanilla, sour cream and egg yolk until it becomes smooth in a separate bowl. Mix in the flour mixture.
2. Cut the dough into 4 parts. Form each into disk then wrap with plastic. Put it in the refrigerator until it becomes firm or for 30 minutes.
3. Heat the oven beforehand to 350 degrees. Combine extract, almonds, coconut and raspberry jam until mixed in a small bowl. Make a 10-inch circle by rolling each part of dough on a well-sugared surface. On top of the circles, spread about 1/3 cup of filling then cut each into 12 wedges. Roll the wedges up from the wide ends then put on parchment paper-lined baking sheets, point side down, leaving 1-inch space apart. Form crescents by curving the dough. Brush egg white and use coarse sugar to sprinkle.
4. Bake until set or for 15 to 18 minutes; avoid browning. Allow to cool by transferring to wire racks from the pans.

Red & Green Pinwheels

Serving: *6 dozen. | Prep: 30m | Ready in: 30m*

Ingredients

- 10 tbsps. butter, softened
- 1/2 cup packed brown sugar
- 1/4 cup granulated sugar
- 1 large egg
- 1/2 tsp. peppermint extract
- 2 cups all-purpose flour
- 1/2 tsp. baking powder
- 1/2 tsp. salt
- 1/8 tsp. baking soda
- 1/2 tsp. red gel food coloring
- 1/4 tsp. green gel food coloring

Direction

1. Heat the oven beforehand to 375 degrees. Cream the sugars and butter until fluffy and light. Stir in extract and egg. Whisk baking soda, salt, baking powder and flour in a different bowl then put in the creamed mixture gradually. Mix well.
2. Cut the dough into 2 parts. Tint one part with green and red for the other. Cut each part into 2, making 4 doughs altogether. Roll each into 9x6-inch rectangle between sheets of waxed paper. Put in the refrigerator for 15 minutes.
3. Discard the waxed paper then put one green dough on top of one red dough. Tightly roll up, starting with the long side, in jelly-roll style; wrap with plastic. Repeat then put in the refrigerator for about an hour until firm.
4. Remove the wrap then slice into 1/4-inch slices crosswise. Put on baking sheets without grease, leaving 1-inch space apart. Bake for 7 to 9 minutes until set. Allow to cool by putting on wire racks.

Nutrition Information: Calories: 36 calories Total Carbohydrate: 5 g Cholesterol: 7 mg Total Fat: 2 g Fiber: 0 g Protein: 0 g Sodium: 36 mg

Red Velvet Cookies

Serving: 36 | Prep: 30m | Ready in: 40m

Ingredients

- 2 cups all-purpose flour
- 1/2 tsp. baking soda
- 1/2 tsp. salt
- 2 (1 oz.) squares unsweetened baking chocolate, broken into pieces
- 1/2 cup unsalted butter, softened
- 2/3 cup brown sugar, firmly packed
- 1/3 cup white sugar
- 1 large egg
- 1 tbsp. red food coloring
- 3/4 cup sour cream
- 1 cup semisweet chocolate chips (optional)
- Cream Cheese Frosting
- 1/4 cup unsalted butter, softened
- 4 oz. cream cheese, at room temperature
- 1/2 tsp. vanilla extract
- 2 cups confectioners' sugar, sifted

Direction

1. Preheat an oven to 190°C/375°F with rack in center position. Grease/line parchment paper on baking sheets; sift salt, baking soda and flour together.
2. Break chocolate squares to chunks; put in microwave-safe bowl. Microwave for 90 seconds on high till chocolate melts; mix chocolate till smooth. Put aside; cool.
3. Beat white sugar, brown sugar and 1/2 cup butter till fluffy and light in big bowl; put egg in. Beat till smooth. Mix chocolate and red food coloring in, regularly scraping down bowl, for 30 seconds till blended evenly. Add 1/2 sifted dry ingredients; mix till incorporated well. Beat sour cream in; mix

leftover dry ingredients in. Fold chocolate chips in; drop spoonfuls of dough on prepped baking sheets, 2-in. apart.

4. 1 sheet at a time, bake in preheated oven for 9 minutes till they spring back when pressed. Cool for 5 minutes in pans; transfer to completely cool on wire rack.

5. Cream cheese frosting: Whip vanilla, cream cheese and 1/4 cup butter till smooth; in half cup portions, blend powdered sugar in till frosting reaches desired consistency.

Nutrition Information: Calories: 162 calories; Total Carbohydrate: 8 g Cholesterol: 21 mg Total Fat: 4 g Protein: 7 g Sodium: 66 mg

Almond-butter Cookie Bouquet

Serving: about 2-1/2 dozen. | Prep: 02h00m | Ready in: 02h10m

Ingredients

- 1-1/4 cups butter, softened
- 1-3/4 cups confectioners' sugar
- 2 oz. almond paste
- 1 egg
- 1/4 cup 2% milk
- 1 tsp. vanilla extract
- 4 cups all-purpose flour
- 1/2 tsp. salt
- Wooden skewers or lollipop sticks
- ICING:
- 1 cup confectioners' sugar
- 4 tsps. evaporated milk
- Food coloring of your choice

Direction

1. Cream the confectioners' sugar and butter until fluffy and light in a big bowl. Put almond paste in. Stir in vanilla, milk and egg. Mix salt and flour; put in the creamed mixture gradually. Stir well. Cover and put in the refrigerator for an hour.

2. Heat the oven beforehand to 375 degrees. Make 1/4-inch thickness dough by rolling on a lightly floured surface with. Slice out using 3-inch cookie cutters with flour. Put on baking sheets without grease, leaving 1-inch apart; insert sticks or skewers. Bake until firm or for 7 to 8 minutes. Allow to rest for 2 minutes. Transfer to wire racks to cool.

3. Whisk milk and confectioners' sugar in a bowl. Cut into small bowls then tint using food coloring. Spread the icing gently on top of cooled cookies. If desired, decorate using other colors of icing.

Nutrition Information: Calories: 184 calories Total Carbohydrate: 25 g Cholesterol: 28 mg Total Fat: 9 g Fiber: 1 g Protein: 2 g Sodium: 121 mg

Be-mine Sandwich Cookies

Serving: 50-55 cookies. | Prep: 20m | Ready in: 20m

Ingredients

- 6 oz. white or milk chocolate candy coating, coarsely chopped
- 50 to 55 Oreo cookies
- Assorted candy sprinkles or decorations

Direction

1. Melt 2-oz. candy coating at one time in microwave; mix till smooth. Spread on cookie tops; immediately decorate. Put on waxed paper till set.

Nutrition Information: Calories: 65 calories Total Carbohydrate: 9 g Cholesterol: 0 mg Total Fat: 3 g Fiber: 0 g Protein: 1 g Sodium: 67 mg

Berry-almond Sandwich Cookies

Serving: 3 dozen. | Prep: 30m | Ready in: 40m

Ingredients

- 1-1/2 cups butter, softened
- 1 cup sugar
- 1 tsp. vanilla extract
- 2-3/4 cups all-purpose flour
- 1/2 tsp. salt
- 2 cups ground almonds
- 3/4 cup raspberry filling
- Edible glitter or confectioners' sugar

Direction

1. Preheat an oven to 325°. Cream sugar and butter till fluffy and light in big bowl; beat vanilla in. Mix salt and flour; add to creamed mixture slowly. Stir well; mix almonds in.
2. Roll dough out to 1/8-in. thick on heavily floured surface. Cut to desired shapes using floured 2 1/2-in. cookie cutters.
3. Put on ungreased baking sheets, 1-in. apart. Bake till edges start to brown, about 10-12 minutes. Transfer to wire racks; cool.
4. Spread 1 tsp. raspberry filling on bottoms of 1/2 of the cookies; top with leftover cookies. Sprinkle confectioners' sugar/edible glitter. Keep in airtight container.

Nutrition Information: Calories: 167 calories Total Carbohydrate: 17 g Cholesterol: 20 mg Total Fat: 10 g Fiber: 1 g Protein: 2 g Sodium: 114 mg

Brandy Snap Cannoli

Serving: about 2 dozen. | Prep: 01h30m | Ready in: 01h35m

Ingredients

- 1/2 cup butter, cubed
- 1/2 cup sugar
- 3 tbsps. molasses
- 1 tsp. ground ginger
- 1/4 tsp. salt
- 1 cup all-purpose flour
- 2 tbsps. brandy
- FILLING:
- 1-1/2 cups ricotta cheese
- 3 tbsps. grated orange zest
- 3 tbsps. sugar, divided
- 1-1/2 cups miniature semisweet chocolate chips, divided
- 1-1/2 cups heavy whipping cream

Direction

1. Mix the first 5 ingredients in a small saucepan. Cook and stir until butter is melted over medium heat. Take off heat. Mix in brandy and flour; keep warm.
2. Drop tablespoonfuls of batter on well-greased or parchment paper-lined baking sheet. Make 4-inchcircle by spreading each batter. Bake until edges begins to turn brown or for 5 to 6 minutes at 350 degrees. Allow to cool just until cookie begins to firm or for about a minute.
3. Do this step quickly. Loosen every cookie and shape by curling around a metal cannoli tube. Remove cookies from the tubes and allow to cool on wire racks.
4. Make the filling by mixing 1 tbsp. of sugar, orange zest and ricotta in a big bowl. Mix 1/2 cup chocolate chips in. Beat the cream until get soft peaks formed on medium speed in a small bowl. Put the remaining sugar gradually while beating on high until get stiff pcaks formed. Fold into ricotta mixture then put in the refrigerator until serving.
5. Pipe the filling into cannoli shells just prior to serving. Dunk ends in the leftover chocolate chips.

Nutrition Information: Calories: 230 calories Total Carbohydrate: 22 g Cholesterol: 40 mg Total Fat: 15 g Fiber: 1 g Protein: 3 g Sodium: 85 mg

Brownie Bourbon Bites

Serving: about 2 dozen. | Prep: 25m | Ready in: 35m

Ingredients

- 1/2 cup butter, softened
- 1/2 cup packed brown sugar
- 1/4 cup bourbon
- 1 cup all-purpose flour
- 3 tbsps. baking cocoa
- 1/2 cup miniature semisweet chocolate chips
- 1 cup coarsely chopped pecans

Direction

1. Cream brown sugar and butter till fluffy and light in small bowl; beat bourbon in. Mix cocoa and flour; add to creamed mixture slowly. Beat till smooth; mix chocolate chips in. Cover; refrigerate for 1-2 hours.
2. Form to 1/2-in balls then roll in pecans; put on ungreased baking sheets, 2-in. apart. Bake for 8-10 minutes at 350° till cookies set; cool for 5 minutes. Transfer from pans carefully onto wire racks; completely cool. Keep in airtight container.

Nutrition Information: Calories: 110 calories Total Carbohydrate: 10 g Cholesterol: 9 mg Total Fat: 7 g Fiber: 1 g Protein: 1 g Sodium: 35 mg

Buttery Potato Chip Cookies

Serving: 4-1/2 dozen. | Prep: 15m | Ready in: 25m

Ingredients

• 2 cups butter, softened
• 1 cup sugar
• 1 tsp. vanilla extract
• 3-1/2 cups all-purpose flour
• 2 cups crushed potato chips
• 3/4 cup chopped walnuts

Direction

1. Preheat an oven to 350°. Cream sugar and butter till fluffy and light in big bowl; beat vanilla in. Add flour slowly to creamed mixture; stir well. Mix walnuts and potato chips in.
2. By rounded tablespoonfuls, drop on ungreased baking sheets, 2-in. apart. Bake till lightly browned, about 10-12 minutes. Cool for 2 minutes. Transfer from pans onto wire racks.

Nutrition Information: Calories: 126 calories Total Carbohydrate: 11 g Cholesterol: 18 mg Total Fat: 9 g Fiber: 0 g Protein: 1 g Sodium: 67 mg

Candied Cherry Hermits

Serving: about 3-1/2 dozen. | Prep: 15m | Ready in: 25m

Ingredients

• 1/2 cup butter, softened
• 1 cup packed brown sugar
• 2 eggs
• 1-1/2 cups all-purpose flour
• 1 to 2 tsps. ground cinnamon
• 1/2 tsp. baking soda
• 1 cup chopped pecans
• 3/4 cup raisins, chopped
• 3/4 cup candied cherries, chopped

Direction

1. Cream brown sugar and butter till fluffy and light in big bowl; one by one, add eggs, beating well with every addition. Mix baking soda, cinnamon and flour; add to creamed mixture slowly. Stir well; mix cherries, raisins and pecans in.
2. By rounded tablespoonfuls, drop on ungreased baking sheets, 2-in. apart. Bake for 10-12 minutes at 375° till golden brown. Transfer to wire racks; cool.

Nutrition Information: Calories: 191 calories Total Carbohydrate: 27 g Cholesterol: 32 mg Total Fat: 9 g Fiber: 1 g Protein: 2 g Sodium: 90 mg

Chai Snickerdoodles

Serving: 6-1/2 dozen. | Prep: 30m | Ready in: 40m

Ingredients

- 2 cups sugar
- 2 tsps. ground cinnamon
- 1 tsp. ground ginger
- 1 tsp. ground cardamom
- 1/2 tsp. ground allspice
- 1 cup butter, softened
- 2 eggs
- 1-1/2 tsps. vanilla extract
- 2-3/4 cups all-purpose flour
- 2 tsps. cream of tartar
- 1 tsp. baking soda
- 1/8 tsp. salt

Direction

1. Mix allspice, cardamom, ginger, cinnamon and sugar in small bowl; take 1/2 cup sugar mixture to shallow bowl. Put aside.
2. Cream leftover sugar mixture and butter till fluffy and light in big bowl; beat vanilla and eggs in. Mix salt, baking soda, cream of tartar and flour; add to creamed mixture slowly. Stir well.
3. Form to 1 1/2-in. balls then roll in reserved sugar mixture. Put on parchment paper-lined baking sheets, 2-in. apart. Bake for 10-13 minutes till edges start to brown at 350°; cool for 2 minutes. Transfer from pans onto wire racks.

Nutrition Information: Calories: 59 calories Total Carbohydrate: 9 g Cholesterol: 12 mg Total Fat: 3 g Fiber: 0 g Protein: 1 g Sodium: 38 mg

Cherry Bonbon Cookies

Serving: 2 dozen. | Prep: 15m | Ready in: 35m

Ingredients

- 1/2 cup butter, softened
- 3/4 cup confectioners' sugar
- 2 tbsps. milk
- 1 tsp. vanilla extract
- 1-1/2 cups all-purpose flour
- 1/8 tsp. salt
- 24 maraschino cherries
- GLAZE:
- 1 cup confectioners' sugar
- 1 tbsp. butter, melted
- 2 tbsps. maraschino cherry juice
- Additional confectioners' sugar

Direction Serving:

1. Heat the oven beforehand to 350 degrees. Cream the sugar and butter until fluffy and light in a big bowl. Put vanilla and milk. Mix salt and flour; put in the creamed mixture gradually.
2. Cut the dough into 24 parts. Form a ball by shaping every part around one cherry. Put them on baking sheets without grease. Bake until lightly browned or for 18 to 20 minutes. Allow to cool by putting on wire racks.
3. For the glaze, mix cherry juice, butter and sugar until smooth. Sprinkle on top of the cookies. Dust using confectioners' sugar.

Nutrition Information: Calories: 113 calories Total Carbohydrate: 18 g Cholesterol: 12 mg Total Fat: 4 g Fiber: 0 g Protein: 1 g Sodium: 48 mg

Cherry Cordial Cookies

Serving: 12

Ingredients

- 1 cup dried cherries
- 1/3 cup cherry liqueur
- 1/2 cup unsalted butter
- 1/2 cup white sugar
- 1/2 cup packed brown sugar
- 1 egg
- 1 1/2 tsps. vanilla extract
- 1 tsp. almond extract
- 1 1/2 cups all-purpose flour
- 1/2 tsp. baking soda
- 3/4 cup chopped white chocolate
- 1/2 cup chopped semisweet chocolate
- 1/2 cup chopped macadamia nuts

Direction

1. Dip the dried cherries for 2 to 3 minutes in boiling water. Drain then soak in a small bowl with cherry liqueur. The longer you soak dried cherries, the better you get. Heat the oven beforehand to 175°C or 350°F. Arrange parchment paper on the cookie sheets.
2. Cream the brown sugar and white sugar in butter in a medium bowl. Mix in almond extract, vanilla and egg. Sift the baking soda and the flour together then stir into the mixture that was creamed. Fold the cherries mixture in gently, with the macadamia nuts, semi-sweet chocolate, white chocolate and liqueur. The batter will become creamy and soft.
3. By tbsps., drop the cookie dough onto prepped cookie sheet, 2 to 3 inches of space between cookie sheet. Bake it in the preheated oven for 12 to 13 minutes. The cookies should turn lightly browned. Transfer to wire racks from baking sheets; allow to cool.

Nutrition Information: Calories: 394 calories; Total Carbohydrate: 3 g Cholesterol: 38 mg Total Fat: 2 g Protein: 5 g Sodium: 74 mg

Cherry Kisses

Serving: 6 dozen. | *Prep: 10m* | *Ready in: 30m*

Ingredients

- 4 large egg whites
- 1-1/4 cups sugar
- 1/3 cup chopped walnuts
- 1/3 cup chopped pitted dates
- 1/3 cup chopped candied cherries

Direction

1. Put egg whites in big bowl; stand for 30 minutes at room temperature. Beat till soft peaks form on medium speed. 1 tbsp. at a time, beat in sugar slowly on high till sugar melts and stiff glossy peaks form; fold cherries, dates and walnuts in.
2. Drop on lightly greased baking sheets, 2-in. apart, by teaspoonfuls. Bake for 20-30 minutes till firm to touch at 300°. Cool for 1 minute; remove onto wire rack. Keep in airtight container.

Nutrition Information: Calories: 45 calories Total Carbohydrate: 10 g Cholesterol: 0 mg Total Fat: 1 g Fiber: 0 g Protein: 1 g Sodium: 7 mg

Cherry No-bake Cookies

Serving: about 5-1/2 dozen. | *Prep: 30m* | *Ready in: 30m*

Ingredients

- 2 cups sugar
- 1/2 cup butter, cubed
- 6 tbsps. 2% milk
- 3 tbsps. baking cocoa
- 1 cup peanut butter

- 1/2 tsp. vanilla extract
- 1/4 tsp. almond extract
- 3 cups quick-cooking oats
- 1 jar (10 oz.) maraschino cherries, well drained and finely chopped

Direction

1. Mix cocoa, milk, butter and sugar in a big saucepan. Let to boil while constantly stirring. Cook and mix for 3 minutes.
2. Make off heat. Mix in extracts and peanut butter until combined. Mix in cherries and oats; by tablespoonfuls, drop the mixture on baking sheets lined with waxed paper. Put in the refrigerator until set; keep in airtight containers.

Nutrition Information: Calories: 81 calories Total Carbohydrate: 11 g Cholesterol: 4 mg Total Fat: 4 g Fiber: 1 g Protein: 2 g Sodium: 29 mg

Cherry Pinwheel Cookies

Serving: about 5 dozen. | Prep: 30m | Ready in: 40m

Ingredients

- 3/4 cup butter, softened
- 1 cup sugar
- 1 large egg
- 1 tsp. vanilla extract
- 2 cups all-purpose flour
- 1/2 tsp. baking powder
- 1/4 tsp. salt
- 2 tsps. cherry extract or cherry brandy
- Red paste food coloring
- 1/4 cup ground almonds
- Coarse sugar

Direction

1. Cream sugar and butter till fluffy and light in big bowl; beat vanilla and egg in. Whisk salt, baking powder and flour in separate bowl; beat into creamed mixture slowly. Refrigerate for 1 hour, covered.
2. Halve dough; add cherry extract to 1 half and tint red. Knead almonds into leftover half. Use plastic to wrap each; refrigerate till firm enough to roll, about a minimum of 3 hours.
3. Roll each portion between 2 waxed paper sheets to 15x8-in. rectangle on baking sheet; refrigerate for 30 minutes.
4. Remove the waxed paper; put almond rectangle over cherry rectangle. Tightly roll up, beginning with long side, jellyroll style. In coarse sugar, roll; use plastic to wrap. Refrigerate till firm, 2 hours.
5. Preheat an oven to 375°. Unwrap; crosswise, cut dough to 1/4-in. slices. Put on greased baking sheets, 2-in. apart. Bake till set, about 10-12 minutes. Transfer from pans onto wire racks; completely cool. Keep in airtight containers.

Nutrition Information: Calories: 105 calories Total Carbohydrate: 13 g Cholesterol: 18 mg Total Fat: 5 g Fiber: 0 g Protein: 1 g Sodium: 67 mg

Cranberry Swirl Biscotti

Serving: about 2-1/2 dozen. | Prep: 20m | Ready in: 60m

Ingredients

• 2/3 cup dried cranberries
• 1/2 cup cherry preserves
• 1/2 tsp. ground cinnamon
• 1/2 cup butter, softened
• 2/3 cup sugar
• 2 large eggs
• 1 tsp. vanilla extract
• 2-1/4 cups all-purpose flour
• 3/4 tsp. baking powder
• 1/4 tsp. salt
• GLAZE:
• 3/4 cup confectioners' sugar
• 1 tbsp. 2% milk
• 2 tsps. butter, melted
• 1 tsp. almond extract

Direction

1. Preheat an oven to 325°. Process cinnamon, preserves and cranberries till smooth in food processor.
2. Cream sugar and butter till fluffy and light in big bowl; beat vanilla and eggs in. Whisk salt, baking powder and flour in separate bowl; beat into creamed mixture slowly.
3. Halve dough; roll every dough portion to 12x8-in. rectangle on lightly floured surface. Spread each with 1/2 cranberry mixture; beginning at a short side, roll up like a jellyroll.
4. Put rolls, seam side down, on lightly greased baking sheet, 4-in. apart. Bake till light brown, 25-30 minutes.
5. Put rolls carefully onto cutting board; cool for 5 minutes. Cut crosswise into 1/2-in. slices with a serrated knife. Put slices on lightly greased baking sheets, upright.
6. Bake till centers are dry and firm, about 15-20 minutes more. Transfer from pans onto wire racks.
7. Mix glaze ingredients in small bowl; drizzle on warm cookies. Completely cool. Keep in airtight container.

Nutrition Information: Calories: 120 calories Total Carbohydrate: 20 g Cholesterol: 23 mg Total Fat: 4 g Fiber: 0 g Protein: 1 g Sodium: 58 mg

Cranberry Tea Cookies

Serving: 50 cookies. | Prep: 40m | Ready in: 60m

Ingredients

- 1/2 cup butter, softened
- 4 oz. cream cheese, softened
- 1/3 cup plus 1/2 cup sugar, divided
- 1/4 tsp. salt
- 1-1/4 cups all-purpose flour
- 1-1/4 cups dried cranberries, chopped
- 1 tsp. grated orange zest
- 1/2 cup orange juice
- Confectioners' sugar

Direction

1. Whip together in a large bowl the salt, 1/3 cup sugar, cream cheese and butter. Slowly add in the flour. Split dough in half. Form each dough portion into a disk; use plastic wrap to wrap. Place inside the refrigerator for 1 hour or until solid enough to roll. Combine together in small heavy saucepan the left sugar, orange juice, orange zest, and cranberries. Make it boil. Lower the heat; gently boil without cover for 8-10 minutes or until liquid is nearly absorbed, stirring from time to time. Let it cool fully. Prepare the oven by preheating to 325 degrees F. Roll each piece of dough into a 10-in. square on a floured surface. Slice into twenty-five 2-in. Squares each. Put 1 tsp. cranberry mixture in the middle of each square. Take two opposite corners of each square to the middle; seal by pinching firmly. On greased baking sheets, put squares 1 in. apart. Place inside the preheated oven for 18-20 minutes or until edges are golden brown in color. Take from pans and put on wire racks and cool fully. Sprinkle confectioner's sugar on tops.

Nutrition Information: Calories: 62 calories Total Carbohydrate: 9 g Cholesterol: 7 mg Total Fat: 3 g Fiber: 0 g Protein: 1 g Sodium: 34 mg

Crinkle-top Chocolate Cookies

Serving: *about 3-1/2 dozen. | Prep: 15m | Ready in: 25m*

Ingredients

- 2 cups (about 12 oz.) semisweet chocolate chips, divided
- 2 tbsps. butter, softened
- 1 cup sugar
- 2 large egg whites
- 1-1/2 tsps. vanilla extract
- 1-1/2 cups all-purpose flour
- 1-1/2 tsps. baking powder
- 1/4 tsp. salt
- 1/4 cup water
- 1/2 cup confectioners' sugar

Direction

1. Melt 1 cup chocolate chips in microwave. Mix till smooth; put aside. Beat sugar and butter for 2 minutes till crumbly. Add vanilla and egg whites; beat well. Mix melted chocolate in.
2. Whisk salt, baking powder and flour in separate bowl; alternately with water, add to butter mixture slowly. Mix leftover chocolate chips in. Refrigerate for 2 hours till easy to handle, covered.
3. Preheat an oven to 350°; form dough to 1-in. balls then roll in confectioners' sugar. Put on baking sheets that are coated in cooking spray, 2-in. apart. Bake for 10-12 minutes till set. Transfer to wire racks; cool.

Nutrition Information: Calories: 85 calories Total Carbohydrate: 15 g Cholesterol: 1 mg Total Fat: 3 g Fiber: 1 g Protein: 1 g Sodium: 39 mg

Crisp Lemon Tea Cookies

Serving: 2 dozen. | Prep: 40m | Ready in: 50m

Ingredients

- 1/2 cup butter, softened
- 1/2 cup sugar
- 1 tbsp. 2% milk
- 1/2 tsp. vanilla extract
- 1-1/4 cups all-purpose flour
- 1/2 tsp. ground cinnamon
- FROSTING:
- 2 tbsps. plus 1 tsp. butter
- 1-1/2 cups confectioners' sugar
- 2 tbsps. lemon juice
- Assorted M&M's miniature baking bits

Direction

1. Cream the sugar and butter until fluffy and light in a small bowl. Beat in vanilla and milk. Mix cinnamon and flour then put to the creamed mixture gradually. Stir well. Make an 8x2-inch roll out of the dough then wrap using plastic. Put in the freezer.
2. Unwrap the cookie dough and allow to sit for 10 minutes at room temperature to use the frozen cookie dough. Chop into 1/4 inch slices then put on baking sheets without grease, leaving 2 inches space apart. Let to bake at 375° till browned lightly or for 8 to 10 minutes. Allow to cool by putting on wire racks.
3. Cream the confectioners' sugar and butter until fluffy and light in a separate small bowl to make the frosting. Beat in the lemon juice gradually; frost the cookies. Use baking bits to decorate.

Nutrition Information: Calories: 113 calories Total Carbohydrate: 17 g Cholesterol: 13 mg Total Fat: 5 g Fiber: 0 g Protein: 1 g Sodium: 35 mg

Cupcake Cookie Pops

Serving: 2 dozen. | Prep: 60m | Ready in: 01h15m

Ingredients

- 1 tube (16-1/2 oz.) refrigerated sugar cookie dough
- 2/3 cup all-purpose flour
- Lollipop sticks or pretzel sticks
- Jolly Rancher hard candies, coarsely crushed
- ROYAL ICING:
- 1-1/2 cups confectioners' sugar
- 2 tbsps. water
- 3-1/4 tsps. meringue powder
- Dash cream of tartar
- Food coloring, optional

Direction

1. Preheat an oven to 350°. Beat flour and cookie dough till blended. Roll dough out to 1/4-in. thick on lightly floured surface; use cookie cutters of your preference dipped in flour to cut out.
2. Lollipop cookies: Put pretzel sticks/lollipop sticks on foil-lined baking sheets; put cutout dough over each. Gently press down. Bake for 9-11 minutes till light browned. Transfer to wire racks carefully; cool.
3. Cutouts with candy centers: Put cutouts on foil-lined baking sheets, 1-in. apart. Cut center of every cookie out; bake for 9-11 minutes. Put crushed candy in middles; bake for 3-5 more minutes till lightly browned. Completely cool; transfer to wire racks carefully.
4. Frosted cookies: Put cutouts on foil-lined baking sheets; bake for 9-11 minutes till lightly browned. Transfer to wire racks; cool.
5. Meanwhile, for royal icing, beat cream of tartar, meringue powder, water and confectioners' sugar on low speed till just combined; beat for 4-5 minutes on high till stiff peaks form. If desired, tint with food coloring. Cut small hole in tip of a pastry bag/corner of a food-safe plastic bag. Put icing in bag; use damp cloth to cover unused icing at all times. Beat again to restore texture on high speed if needed.
6. Use plain icing to outline each cookie; dry. Use tinted icing to fill middle of every cookie. Spread using a toothpick; completely dry. Attach decorations and candies with extra icing.

Cutout Wedding Cookies

Serving: about 4 dozen. | Prep: 50m | Ready in: 60m

Ingredients

- 3/4 cup butter, softened
- 1 cup sugar
- 2 large eggs
- 1 tsp. almond extract
- 2-1/2 cups all-purpose flour
- 1 tsp. baking powder
- 1 tsp. salt
- FROSTING:
- 1/2 cup butter, softened
- 4-1/2 cups confectioners' sugar
- 1-1/2 tsps. vanilla extract

- 5 to 6 tbsps. 2% milk
- Paste food coloring of your choice
- Edible glitter and colored sugar
- Sprinkles, optional

Direction

1. Cream the sugar and butter until fluffy and light in a big bowl. Beat the extract and eggs in. Mix salt, flour and baking powder then put into the creamed mixture gradually. Stir well. Cover and put in the refrigerator until easy to handle or for an hour.
2. Make 1/4-inch thickness dough by rolling it out on a well-floured surface. Use a 2 1/2-inch to 4-inchlove-themed cookie cutters to cut the dough. Put the dough 2 inches apart on baking sheets with grease. Bake until set or for 6 to 8 minutes at 400 degrees. Allow to cool completely by putting into wire racks.
3. Beat butter until fluffy and light in a big bowl to make the frosting. Beat in the vanilla, confectioners' sugar and milk to get your preferred consistency. Color the frosting as you prefer then frost the cookies. Mix same amounts of colored sugar and edible glitter then sprinkle on cookies. If preferred, decorate some cookies with sprinkles.

Nutrition Information: Calories: 130 calories Total Carbohydrate: 20 g Cholesterol: 21 mg Total Fat: 5 g Fiber: 0 g Protein: 1 g Sodium: 95 mg

Decorated Butter Cookies

Serving: 4 dozen. | Prep: 20m | Ready in: 30m

Ingredients

- 1 cup butter, softened
- 1/2 cup sugar
- 1/2 cup packed brown sugar
- 1 egg
- 1 tsp. vanilla extract
- 2 cups all-purpose flour
- 2 tsps. cream of tartar
- 1 tsp. baking soda
- 1/8 tsp. salt
- Colored sprinkles, colored sugar, ground nuts and/or chocolate sprinkles

Direction

1. Cream the sugars and butter until fluffy and light in a small bowl. Beat in vanilla and egg. Mix salt, baking soda, cream of tartar and flour; put in the creamed mixture gradually. Stir well. Cover and put in the refrigerator until easy to handle or for an hour.
2. Make 1-inch balls by rolling the dough. Put on baking sheets without grease, leaving 2-inch space apart. Flatten using a glass dipped in sugar then sprinkle using nuts, colored sugar or sprinkles.
3. Bake until lightly browned or for 10 to 12 minutes at 350 degrees. Allow to cool by putting on wire

racks.

Nutrition Information: Calories: 142 calories Total Carbohydrate: 17 g Cholesterol: 29 mg Total Fat: 8 g Fiber: 0 g Protein: 1 g Sodium: 147 mg

Dipped Cherry Cookies

Serving: about 4 dozen. | Prep: 30m | Ready in: 40m

Ingredients

- 2-1/2 cups all-purpose flour
- 3/4 cup sugar, divided
- 1 cup cold butter, cubed
- 1/2 cup finely chopped maraschino cherries, patted dry
- 12 oz. white baking chocolate, finely chopped, divided
- 1/2 tsp. almond extract
- 2 tsps. shortening
- Coarse sugar and red edible glitter

Direction

1. Mix half cup of sugar and flour in a big bowl. Cut butter in until crumbly. Knead in the extract, 2/3 cup of white chocolate and cherries until the dough forms a ball.
2. Form into 3/4-inch balls; put them on baking sheets without grease, leaving 2-inch space apart. Slightly flatten using a glass that was dipped in the leftover sugar. Bake until edges turn light brown or for 10 to 12 minutes at 325 degrees. Allow to cool completely by putting on wire racks.
3. Melt remaining white chocolate and shortening in a microwave then mix until smooth.
4. Dunk half of every cookie in the chocolate; let excess drip off. Put on waxed paper and use edible glitter and coarse sugar to sprinkle. Let rest until set and keep in an airtight container.

Nutrition Information: Calories: 108 calories Total Carbohydrate: 12 g Cholesterol: 11 mg Total Fat: 6 g Fiber: 0 g Protein: 1 g Sodium: 34 mg

Double Chocolate Chip Cookies

Serving: 3-4 dozen. | Prep: 25m | Ready in: 35m

Ingredients

- 1 cup butter, softened
- 1 cup granulated sugar
- 1/2 cup packed dark brown sugar
- 1 tsp. vanilla extract
- 1 large egg
- 1/3 cup baking cocoa
- 2 tbsps. whole milk
- 1-3/4 cups all-purpose flour

- 1/4 tsp. baking powder
- 1 cup chopped walnuts
- 1 cup (6 oz.) semisweet chocolate chips

Direction

1. Preheat an oven to 350°. Cream vanilla, sugars and butter; beat egg in. Add milk and cocoa. Whisk baking powder and flour; fold into creamed mixture with chocolate chips and walnuts; refrigerate for 30 minutes.
2. Roll rounded tablespoonfuls of dough to balls; put on ungreased baking sheets, 2-in. apart. Bake for 10-12 minutes till set. Cool on pans for 5 minutes; transfer to wire racks to completely cool.

Nutrition Information: Calories: 334 calories Total Carbohydrate: 38 g Cholesterol: 44 mg Total Fat: 20 g Fiber: 2 g Protein: 5 g Sodium: 131 mg

Double Chocolate Chipotle Cookies

Serving: 1-1/2 dozen. | Prep: 25m | Ready in: 35m

Ingredients

- 2/3 cup butter, softened
- 1/2 cup sugar
- 1/2 cup packed brown sugar
- 1 egg
- 1 tsp. vanilla extract
- 1/2 tsp. minced chipotle pepper in adobo sauce
- 1 cup plus 2 tbsps. all-purpose flour
- 1/3 cup baking cocoa
- 1 tsp. ground cinnamon
- 1/2 tsp. salt
- 1/2 tsp. baking soda
- 1/4 tsp. cayenne pepper
- 3 milk chocolate candy bars (55 oz. each), chopped
- Confectioners' sugar

Direction

1. Cream sugars and butter till fluffy and light in big bowl; beat chipotle pepper, vanilla and egg in. Mix cayenne, baking soda, salt, cinnamon, cocoa and flour; add to creamed mixture slowly. Stir well; mix chopped candy in. Chill till easy to handle, 1 hour.
2. Preheat an oven to 350°; roll to 1 1/2-in. balls. Put on ungreased baking sheets, 4-in. apart. Bake till set, about 10-12 minutes; cool for 4 minutes. Transfer from pans onto wire racks; dust confectioners' sugar over.

Nutrition Information: Calories: 179 calories Total Carbohydrate: 23 g Cholesterol: 31 mg Total Fat: 9 g Fiber: 1 g Protein: 2 g Sodium: 161 mg

Double Chocolate, Orange And Hazelnut Biscotti

Serving: about 1-1/2 dozen. | Prep: 20m | Ready in: 45m

Ingredients

- 1/4 cup whole hazelnuts, toasted and skins removed
- 1 large egg
- 1/3 cup sugar
- 1/4 cup 2% milk
- 1 tsp. vanilla extract
- 2 cups all-purpose flour
- 1/4 cup baking cocoa
- 1/4 tsp. baking soda
- Dash salt
- 2 tsps. grated orange zest
- 1/2 cup semisweet chocolate chips

Direction

1. Prepare the oven by preheating to 350°F. In a resealable plastic bag, put the hazelnuts; use a rolling pin or mallet to crush nuts.
2. Whisk milk, sugar, and egg until thick and light; stir in vanilla. Combine salt, baking soda, cocoa, and flour; add in orange zest. Slowly whisk into egg mixture (dough will be thick). Add in crushed hazelnuts and chocolate chips then fold by hand.
3. On a baking sheet that is not greased, form dough into 1 9x5 inch rectangle. Bake in the preheated oven for about 20 minutes until a toothpick pricked in middle comes out clean. Let cool on pans on wire racks for 5-10 minutes until firm.
4. Lower oven setting to 325°F. Place baked rectangle to a cutting board. Cut crosswise into 1/2-inch slices using a serrated knife. Set on baking sheets, cut sides down. Put back to the oven and bake for 6-8 minutes per side until crisp. Take from pans to wire racks to fully cool. Keep in an airtight container.

Nutrition Information: Calories: 112 calories Total Carbohydrate: 19 g Cholesterol: 11 mg Total Fat: 3 g Fiber: 1 g Protein: 3 g Sodium: 105 mg

Frosted Valentine Cookies

Serving: 3-1/2 dozen. | Prep: 25m | Ready in: 40m

Ingredients

- 2 cups butter, softened
- 1 cup confectioners' sugar
- 4 cups all-purpose flour
- 2 cups quick-cooking oats

- 2 tsps. vanilla extract
- 1/2 tsp. almond extract
- 1/2 tsp. salt
- 1/2 lb. dark or milk chocolate candy coating, melted
- Confectioners' sugar icing, optional

Direction

1. Cream sugar and butter till fluffy and light in bowl. Add salt, extracts, oats and flour; stir well.
2. Roll dough out to 1/4-in. thick; use 3-in. heart-shaped cookie cutter to cut. Put on ungreased baking sheets; bake for 12-15 minutes at 350°. Spread candy coating on warm cookies; cool. If desired, decorate with icing.

Nutrition Information: Calories: 349 calories Total Carbohydrate: 36 g Cholesterol: 47 mg Total Fat: 21 g Fiber: 2 g Protein: 4 g Sodium: 233 mg

Gingerbread Oatmeal Cookies

Serving: about 1-1/2 dozen. | Prep: 10m | Ready in: 25m

Ingredients

- 3/4 cup all-purpose flour
- 1/2 tsp. baking soda
- 1/2 tsp. salt
- 1/2 tsp. ground ginger
- 1/4 tsp. baking powder
- 1 cup Biscoff creamy cookie spread, room temperature
- 1/2 cup unsalted butter
- 1/2 cup granulated sugar
- 1/2 cup packed brown sugar
- 1 large egg
- 1 tsp. vanilla extract
- 1 cup quick-cooking oats

Direction

1. Heat oven to 350°. Beat the initial five ingredients together. Whisk the sugars, butter, and cookie spread into a separate bowl until fluffy and light. Stir in vanilla and egg. Slowly stir in the flour mixture and mix in the oats. Keep in refrigerator for a minimum of 3 hours.
2. Bring the dough to room temperature. Drop dough mounds with a medium cookie scoop into the parchment-lined baking pans. For 15 to 18 minutes, bake until cookies turn lightly brown, turning the pans midway through the baking time. For 5 minutes, cool the cookies on the pans. Take out the cookies from the pans and transfer onto wire racks; cool completely.

Nutrition Information: Calories: 210 calories Total Carbohydrate: 26 g Cholesterol: 24 mg Total Fat: 11 g Fiber: 1 g Protein: 2 g Sodium: 113 mg

Glazed Butter Cookies

Serving: about 3 dozen. | Prep: 20m | Ready in: 30m

Ingredients

- 1/2 cup butter, softened
- 3/4 cup sugar
- 1 egg
- 3/4 tsp. vanilla extract
- 1-3/4 cups all-purpose flour
- 1/2 tsp. baking powder
- 1/4 tsp. salt
- GLAZE:
- 1 cup confectioners' sugar
- 1 to 2 tbsps. milk
- Red, green and yellow liquid or paste food coloring

Direction

1. Cream the sugar and butter until fluffy and light in a small bowl. Beat vanilla and egg in. Mix the dry ingredients and put in the creamed mixture gradually. Cover and put in the refrigerator until easy to handle or for an hour.
2. Make 1/8-inch thickness dough by rolling on a lightly floured surface. Cut the dough using 2 1/2-inch cookie cutters; put on baking sheets without grease, leaving 1-inch apart. Bake until lightly browned or for 8 to 10 minutes at 350 degrees. Allow to cool by putting on wire racks.
3. Mix milk and confectioners' sugar until smooth in a small bowl. Mix in food coloring then pour on top of the cooled cookies lightly. Allow to rest until set.

Nutrition Information: Calories: 152 calories Total Carbohydrate: 24 g Cholesterol: 26 mg Total Fat: 5 g Fiber: 0 g Protein: 2 g Sodium: 100 mg

Glazed Cherry Bon Bon Cookies

Serving: 3 dozen. | Prep: 20m | Ready in: 35m

Ingredients

- 36 maraschino cherries
- 1 cup butter, softened
- 1-1/2 cups confectioners' sugar
- 1 tbsp. 2% milk
- 3 tsps. vanilla extract
- 2-3/4 cups all-purpose flour
- 1/4 tsp. salt
- CHRISTMAS GLAZE:

- 1-1/4 cups confectioners' sugar
- 1 to 2 tbsps. water
- Red and green liquid food coloring
- Colored sprinkles
- CHOCOLATE GLAZE:
- 1 oz. unsweetened chocolate, melted
- 1 tsp. vanilla extract
- 1 cup confectioners' sugar
- 1 to 2 tbsps. water
- 1/2 cup chopped pecans or walnuts

Direction

1. Use paper towels to pat dry the cherries. Cream the confectioners' sugar and butter until fluffy and light in a big bowl. Beat in vanilla and milk. Mix salt and flour then put into creamed mixture gradually. Stir well.
2. Form a circle by forming a tablespoonful of dough around each cherry. Put on baking sheets without grease, leaving 2 inches space apart. Bake until the bottoms turn brown or for 14 to 16 minutes at 350 degrees. Allow to cool by putting on wire racks.
3. To make the Christmas glaze: Combine enough water and confectioners' sugar in a small bowl to achieve the consistency of dipping. Put 1/2 of the glaze in a separate bowl then tint one bowl with red color and green color on the other. Dunk the top of 9 cookies in the green glaze and another 9 in the red glaze. Use sprinkles to decorate then let it rest until set.
4. To make the chocolate glaze: Combine enough water and confectioners' sugar in a small bowl to achieve the consistency of the dipping. Mix in vanilla and chocolate. Dunk the top of the rest of the cookies in the glaze. Use nuts to sprinkle then let it rest until set.

Nutrition Information: Calories: 155 calories Total Carbohydrate: 23 g Cholesterol: 13 mg Total Fat: 7 g Fiber: 1 g Protein: 1 g Sodium: 53 mg

Grandma's Sugar Cookies

Serving: 24

Ingredients

- 1 cup packed brown sugar
- 1 cup white sugar
- 4 eggs, beaten
- 1 cup shortening
- 5 cups all-purpose flour
- 1 tbsp. baking powder
- 1 tsp. baking soda
- 2 tsps. ground cinnamon
- 1 tsp. ground nutmeg
- 1 cup buttermilk
- 1/2 cup colored sugar for decoration

Direction

1. Heat the oven beforehand to 175°C or 350°F.
2. Cream the shortening, eggs, white sugar and brown sugar in a big bowl. Sift the nutmeg, cinnamon, baking soda, baking powder and flour together. Put the buttermilk alternately with the dry ingredients.
3. Make walnut sized balls by rolling the dough and if desired, roll the balls in colored sugar. Put on an unprepared cookie sheet, leaving 2-inch space apart. Bake it in the preheated oven for 10 to 13 minutes. Allow to cool by putting on wire racks.

Nutrition Information: Calories: 271 calories; Total Carbohydrate: 3 g Cholesterol: 31 mg Total Fat: 8 g Protein: 1 g Sodium: 139 mg

Halloween Night Cookie Puzzle

Serving: 1 cookie puzzle. | Prep: 30m | Ready in: 50m

Ingredients

- 1 tube (18 oz.) refrigerated sugar cookie dough, softened
- 1/2 cup all-purpose flour
- Unblanched almonds
- 3 cups confectioners' sugar
- 1/3 cup light corn syrup
- 2 to 4 tbsps. water
- Assorted food coloring, decorating gels, sprinkles and candies

Direction

1. Mix flour and cookie dough in big bowl. Roll dough to 14x11-in. rectangle on parchment paper-lined surface. Use Halloween cookie cutters to cut puzzle shapes out; don't remove them. Slide baking sheet under dough and parchment paper; chill for 5 to 10 minutes.
2. Remove shapes; put on ungreased baking sheet. Handles: Press side of almond in middle of every puzzle shape. Bake shapes for 7-9 minutes till edges are golden brown at 350°. While warm, use same cookie cutters to recut shapes to make neat edges. Put in oven till soft if cookies cool too quickly. Transfer to wire racks then cool.
3. Bake big rectangular puzzle on parchment paper-lined baking sheet till edges are golden brown, about 12-13 minutes. Recut shapes inside puzzle immediately to make neat edges. On wire rack, completely cool.
4. Mix water, corn syrup and confectioners' sugar till smooth in small bowl. As desired, use food coloring to tint frosting. Frost shapes and puzzle; decorate with candies, sprinkles and decorating gel as desired. Put puzzle shapes inside the puzzle.

Hazelnut Macarons

Serving: about 5 dozen. | Prep: 50m | Ready in: 60m

Ingredients

- 6 large egg whites
- 1-1/2 cups hazelnuts, toasted
- 2-1/2 cups confectioners' sugar
- Dash salt
- 1/2 cup superfine sugar
- COFFEE BUTTERCREAM:
- 1 cup sugar
- 6 tbsps. water
- 6 large egg yolks
- 4 tsps. instant espresso powder
- 1 tsp. vanilla extract
- 1-1/2 cups butter, softened
- 6 tbsps. confectioners' sugar

Direction

1. In a small bowl, place the egg whites; allow to stand for 30 minutes at room temperature.
2. Prepare the oven by preheating to 350°F. In a food processor, combine confectioner's sugar and hazelnuts; process until nuts are nicely ground.
3. Mix in egg whites and salt; blend on medium speed until form soft peaks. Slowly stir in superfine sugar, 1 tbsp. at a time, blending on high until form stiff peaks. Add in hazelnut mixture then fold.
4. Onto baking sheets that are lined with parchment paper, pipe 1-inch diameter cookies 2-inch apart. Place in the preheated oven and bake for 9-12 minutes until firm to the touch and lightly browned. Place cookies on the parchment paper to wire racks; fully cool.
5. To make the buttercream, mix water and sugar in a heavy saucepan. Make it to a simmer; then cook over medium-high heat until sugar is melted. Separate from heat. Beat a small amount of hot syrup into egg yolks in a small bowl; put all back to the pan, stirring constantly. Cook for 2-3 minutes, until thickened, whisking constantly; separate from heat. Mix in vanilla and espresso powder; fully cool.
6. Whisk butter in a stand mixer with the whisk attachment until creamy. Slowly stir in cooled syrup. Mix in confectioner's sugar until fluffy. Keep in the refrigerator for about 10 minutes, until mixture firms to spreading consistency. Place about 1-1/2 tsp buttercream onto the bottom of each of half of the cookies then spread; put the remaining cookies on top. Keep in an airtight container then refrigerate.

Nutrition Information: Calories: 117 calories Total Carbohydrate: 12 g Cholesterol: 31 mg Total Fat: 8 g Fiber: 0 g Protein: 1 g Sodium: 67 mg

Hazelnut Shortbread Hearts

Serving: 7-1/2 dozen. | Prep: 30m | Ready in: 50m

Ingredients

- 1-1/2 cups butter, softened
- 1 cup confectioners' sugar
- 3 tsps. vanilla extract
- 3 cups all-purpose flour
- 1 cup ground toasted hazelnuts

- 4 oz. bittersweet chocolate, melted
- 2 oz. white baking chocolate, melted

Direction

1. Cream the confectioners' sugar and butter until fluffy and light in a big bowl then mix the vanilla in. Mix hazelnuts and flour then put into the creamed mixture gradually. Stir well. Cover and put in the refrigerator until easy to handle or for an hour.
2. Make 1/4-inch thickness dough by rolling it out on a lightly floured surface. Use a 2-inch floured heat-shaped cookie cutter to cut the dough; put on baking sheets without grease, 1 inch apart.
3. Bake until it turns light brown or for 18 to 20 minutes at 325 degrees. Before letting it completely cool into wire racks, allow it to cool for a minute in the pans.
4. Use bittersweet and white chocolate to drizzle on top of the cookies then let rest until it is set. Keep it in an airtight container.

Nutrition Information: Calories: 63 calories Total Carbohydrate: 6 g Cholesterol: 8 mg Total Fat: 4 g Fiber: 0 g Protein: 1 g Sodium: 22 mg

Heart's Delight Cookies

Serving: 4-1/2 dozen. | Prep: 45m | Ready in: 55m

Ingredients

- 1 cup butter, softened
- 3 cups sugar
- 3 eggs
- 3 tsps. vanilla extract
- 7-1/2 cups all-purpose flour
- 2 tsps. baking powder
- 1 tsp. baking soda
- 1 cup buttermilk
- Coarse sugar, optional
- 54 ribbons (16 inches x 1/8 inch)

Direction

1. Cream sugar and butter in a big bowl then put in eggs, one at a time. Stir it well after every addition. Stir the vanilla in. Mix baking soda, flour and baking powder. Put the flour mixture gradually and alternately with the buttermilk into the creamed mixture. Cover and put in the refrigerator until it is easy to handle or for an hour.
2. Roll the dough out to 1/4 inch thickness on a heavily floured surface. Use a 4 inches heart-shaped cookie cutter with flour to slice the dough. Put the sliced dough on a baking sheet without grease, 1 inch apart. If desired, sprinkle using coarse sugar.
3. Bake until edges are lightly browned or for 8 to 10 minutes at 350 degrees. Before putting to wire racks, allow to cool for 2 minutes. Use straw to poke 2 holes in each cookie while they are still warm. Thread ribbon through the holes and tie a bow when cookies are cooled completely. If necessary, trim the

ribbon.
Nutrition Information: Calories: 142 calories Total Carbohydrate: 25 g Cholesterol: 21 mg Total Fat: 4 g Fiber: 0 g Protein: 2 g Sodium: 81 mg

Heartthrob Cookies

Serving: about 5-1/2 dozen (depending on size). | Prep: 30m | Ready in: 40m

Ingredients

• 2 cups butter-flavored shortening
• 2 cups sugar
• 2 eggs
• 2 tsps. vanilla extract
• 1/4 to 1/2 tsp. peppermint extract
• 4 cups all-purpose flour
• 1 tsp. baking powder
• 1/4 tsp. salt
• 15 drops red food coloring
• Red decorating gel

Direction

1. Cream sugar and shortening in big bowl; one by one, add eggs, beating well with every addition. Beat extracts in. Mix salt, baking powder and flour; add to creamed mixture slowly. Halve dough; tint 1 portion pink. Leave leftover dough white. Cover; refrigerate till easy to handle, 1 hour.
2. Roll each dough portion out to 1/4-in. thick on floured surface; use small heart-shaped cookie cutter that is dipped in flour to cut hearts out.
3. Heart-to-heart cookies: On ungreased baking sheet, put hearts in groups of 3 in straight lines with hearts' sides touching. Bake for 8-10 minutes till edges lightly brown at 375°; transfer to wire racks to let cool then pipe Valentine phrases on the cookies.
4. Valentine wreaths: On ungreased baking sheet, put alternating 6 small hearts' colors in a circle with hearts' sides touching; bake for 8-10 minutes till edges lightly brown at 375°. Transfer to wire racks; cool then pipe Valentine phrases on the cookies.

Nutrition Information: Calories: 214 calories Total Carbohydrate: 24 g Cholesterol: 13 mg Total Fat: 12 g Fiber: 0 g Protein: 2 g Sodium: 34 mg

Holiday Meringue Miniatures

Serving: about 7 dozen. | Prep: 20m | Ready in: 01h20m

Ingredients

• 2 large egg whites, room temperature
• 1/2 tsp. white vinegar
• Dash salt

- 1/2 tsp. almond extract
- 1/2 tsp. vanilla extract
- 1/2 cup granulated sugar
- Red gel food coloring

Direction

1. Heat the oven beforehand to 225 degrees. Beat egg whites with salt and vinegar until doubled in volume and foamy on medium speed. Mix the extracts in. Put sugar in gradually, 1 tbsp. at a time. Every time after you add, beat the mixture on high until sugar dissolves. Keep on beating until get stiff glossy peaks formed.
2. Put a half inch round tip in the pastry bag. Inside the length of pastry bag, paint 5 stripes of red food coloring, then put meringue in pastry bag. Pipe dollops onto the parchment-lined baking sheets, leaving 1-inch space apart.
3. Bake until set and dry for an hour. Turn the oven off and leave the meringues inside for an hour, keeping the oven door closed. Take out and allow to cool completely on baking sheets. Take the meringues out of parchment paper and keep at room temperature in an airtight container.

Nutrition Information: Calories: 5 calories Total Carbohydrate: 1 g Cholesterol: 0 mg Total Fat: 0 g Fiber: 0 g Protein: 0 g Sodium: 19 mg

Homemade Lemon Sugar Cookies

Serving: about 13 dozen. | Prep: 30m | Ready in: 40m

Ingredients

- 2 cups butter, softened
- 4 cups confectioners' sugar
- 4 large eggs
- 3 tbsps. lemon juice
- 3 tbsps. half-and-half cream
- 2 tsps. grated lemon zest
- 6-1/2 cups all-purpose flour
- 1 tsp. baking soda
- 1/4 tsp. salt
- Sugar

Direction

1. Cream confectioners' sugar and butter till fluffy and light in big bowl; one by one, add eggs, beating well with every addition. Beat lemon zest, cream and lemon juice in. Mix salt, baking soda and flour; add to creamed mixture slowly. Cover; refrigerate till easy to handle, about 2 hours.
2. Roll out to 1/8-in. thick on lightly floured surface; use 2 1/2-in. cookie cutters that are dipped in flour to cut. Put on ungreased baking sheets, 1-in. apart; sprinkle sugar over. Bake for 8-10 minutes at 350° till lightly browned. Transfer to wire racks; cool.

Nutrition Information: Calories: 108 calories Total Carbohydrate: 14 g Cholesterol: 24 mg Total Fat: 5 g

Fiber: 0 g Protein: 1 g Sodium: 75 mg

Homemade Macaroon Kisses

Serving: 4 dozen. | Prep: 45m | Ready in: 55m

Ingredients

- 1/3 cup butter, softened
- 3 oz. cream cheese, softened
- 3/4 cup sugar
- 1 large egg yolk
- 2 tsps. almond extract
- 1-1/2 cups all-purpose flour
- 2 tsps. baking powder
- 1/2 tsp. salt
- 5 cups sweetened shredded coconut, divided
- 48 milk chocolate kisses
- Coarse sugar

Direction

1. Cream sugar, cream cheese and butter till fluffy and light in big bowl; beat extract and egg yolk in. Mix salt, baking powder and flour; add to creamed mixture slowly. Stir well; mix 3 cups coconut in. Cover; refrigerate till dough becomes easy to handle, 1 hour.
2. Preheat an oven to 350°; form to 1-in. balls. Roll in leftover coconut; put on ungreased baking sheets, 2-in. apart.
3. Bake till lightly browned, about 10-12 minutes; press chocolate kiss immediately in middle of every cookie. Sprinkle coarse sugar over; cool till chocolate is soft on pan, about 2-3 minutes. Transfer to wire racks; completely cool.

Nutrition Information: Calories: 120 calories Total Carbohydrate: 14 g Cholesterol: 11 mg Total Fat: 7 g Fiber: 1 g Protein: 1 g Sodium: 85 mg

Honey-nut Swirls

Serving: 2 dozen. | Prep: 25m | Ready in: 35m

Ingredients

- 1 sheet frozen puff pastry, thawed
- 1 cup finely chopped walnuts
- 1 cup finely chopped pistachios
- 3 tbsps. brown sugar
- 2 tbsps. butter, softened
- 2 tbsps. honey
- 1 tsp. ground cinnamon

- 1/4 tsp. salt
- 2 tbsps. heavy whipping cream
- 2 tbsps. turbinado (washed raw) sugar or granulated sugar

Direction

1. Unfold puffy pastry on a lightly floured surface. Make a 12x9-inch rectangle by rolling it.
2. Mix salt, cinnamon, honey, butter, brown sugar, pistachios and walnuts in a small bowl. Scatter on the pastry to within half inch of the edges. Roll the pastry jelly-roll style then cut it into half inch slices.
3. Put on parchment paper-lined baking sheets, 2 inches apart. Brush with cream and use sugar to sprinkle. Bake until the color turns light brown or for 10 to 12 minutes at 375 degrees. Transfer to wire racks.

Nutrition Information: Calories: 141 calories Total Carbohydrate: 12 g Cholesterol: 4 mg Total Fat: 10 g Fiber: 2 g Protein: 3 g Sodium: 88 mg

Hot Chocolate Peppermint Cookies

Serving: *about 3-1/2 dozen. | Prep: 30m | Ready in: 40m*

Ingredients

- 1 cup butter, softened
- 1 cup sugar
- 1 large egg
- 1 tsp. peppermint extract
- 2-1/3 cups all-purpose flour
- 1/3 cup baking cocoa
- 1 tsp. salt
- 1 tsp. baking soda
- 1 package (11-1/2 oz.) milk chocolate chips
- 1 cup marshmallow creme
- 1 cup finely crushed peppermint candies

Direction

1. In a big bowl, cream sugar and butter until it becomes fluffy and light; beat the extract and egg in. Mix the baking soda, cocoa powder, salt and flour then put it gradually into the creamed mixture. Stir it well.
2. Put tablespoonful drops of the mixture with 2-inch spaces between on baking sheets with grease. Bake it until the top of cookies are cracked or 10 to 12mins at 375 degrees. Allow it to cool completely by transferring it to wire racks.
3. Melt the chocolate chips in a microwave. Stir the melted chocolate chips until it becomes smooth. Put a drop of teaspoonful of the marshmallow crème in the middle of each cookie. Dip half of each cookie in the melted chocolate and let the excess drip from cookie. Sprinkle candies immediately. Put the cookies on the waxed paper then let it rest until set. Keep in airtight container.

Nutrition Information: Calories: 145 calories Total Carbohydrate: 19 g Cholesterol: 18 mg Total Fat: 7 g Fiber: 1 g Protein: 2 g Sodium: 132 mg

Hugs 'n' Kisses Cookies

Serving: about 5 dozen. | Prep: 15m | Ready in: 25m

Ingredients

• 1 package (18 oz.) refrigerated sugar cookie dough
• Red colored sugar, optional

Direction

1. Cut cookie dough to 1/4-in. slices. Roll each slice to 6-in. rope on floured surface. Cut 1/2 of the ropes widthwise in half. Shape into X's on ungreased baking sheets then seal edges; slightly flatten. Form leftover ropes to O's on ungreased baking sheets then seal edges; slightly flatten. If desired, sprinkle sugar over; bake for 8-10 minutes till edges lightly brown at 350°. Cool for 3 minutes; transfer from pans onto wire racks to completely cool.

Nutrition Information: Calories: 74 calories Total Carbohydrate: 10 g Cholesterol: 5 mg Total Fat: 4 g Fiber: 0 g Protein: 1 g Sodium: 72 mg

Ice Cream Kolachkes

Serving: 10 dozen. | Prep: 60m | Ready in: 01h15m

Ingredients

• 2 cups butter, softened
• 1 pint vanilla ice cream, softened
• 4 cups all-purpose flour
• 2 tbsps. sugar
• 2 cans (12 oz. each) apricot and/or raspberry cake and pastry filling
• 1 to 2 tbsps. confectioners' sugar, optional

Direction

1. Beat ice cream and butter until combined in a bowl of heavy-duty stand mixer. The mixture will seem curdled. Put sugar and flour then stir well. Cut the dough into 4 parts. Cover and put in the refrigerator until easy to handle or for 2 hours.
2. Heat the oven beforehand to 350 degrees. Roll one part of the dough into a 12x10-inch rectangle on a lightly floured surface. Slice the dough into 2-inch squares. In the middle of each square, put 1 teaspoonful of filling overlap the 2 opposite corners of dough on top of the filling. Seal by pinching tightly. Put on ungreased baking sheets, leaving 2-inchspace apart. Repeat with the rest of the dough and filling.
3. Bake it until bottoms are lightly browned or for 11 to 14 minutes. Allow to cool for a minute before transferring to wire racks from the pans. If desired, use confectioners' sugar and sprinkle on top.

Nutrition Information: Calories: 60 calories Total Carbohydrate: 7 g Cholesterol: 9 mg Total Fat: 3 g Fiber: 0 g Protein: 1 g Sodium: 27 mg

Mexican Crinkle Cookies

Serving: about 2 dozen. | Prep: 25m | Ready in: 35m

Ingredients

- 3/4 cup butter, cubed
- 2 oz. unsweetened chocolate, chopped
- 1 cup packed brown sugar
- 1/4 cup light corn syrup
- 1 large egg
- 2 cups all-purpose flour
- 2 tsps. baking soda
- 1-1/2 tsps. ground cinnamon, divided
- 1/4 tsp. salt
- 1/2 cup confectioners' sugar

Direction

1. Melt chocolate and butter in a microwave. Mix until smooth. Mix in corn syrup and brown sugar until combined then stir in egg. Whisk salt, 1 tsp. of cinnamon, baking soda and flour in a separate bowl; mix in the brown sugar mixture gradually. Put in the refrigerator with cover for about an hour until firm.
2. Heat the oven beforehand to 350 degrees. Combine remaining cinnamon and confectioners' sugar in a shallow bowl. Form dough into 1 1/2-inch balls then roll in confectioners' sugar mixture. Put on baking sheets with grease, leaving 2-inchspace apart.
3. Bake for 10 to 12 minutes until tops are cracked and set. Allow to cool on pans; finish cooling by transferring to wire racks.

Nutrition Information: Calories: 158 calories Total Carbohydrate: 22 g Cholesterol: 23 mg Total Fat: 7 g Fiber: 1 g Protein: 2 g Sodium: 184 mg

Michigan Cherry Drops

Serving: about 14 dozen. | Prep: 15m | Ready in: 35m

Ingredients

- 1 cup butter, softened
- 1 cup sugar
- 1/2 cup packed brown sugar
- 4 eggs
- 1-1/2 tsps. vanilla extract
- 4 cups all-purpose flour
- 1 tsp. salt
- 1 tsp. ground cinnamon
- 1/2 tsp. ground nutmeg
- 3-1/2 cups chopped walnuts

- 3 cups chopped maraschino cherries
- 2-2/3 cups raisins

Direction

1. Cream the sugars and butter until fluffy and light in a big bowl. Put eggs in, one at a time. Beat well before putting the next, then beat the vanilla in. Mix nutmeg, cinnamon, salt and flour; put gradually into creamed mixture. Stir well. If necessary, put mixture into in a big bowl. Mix in raisins, cherries and walnuts.
2. Drop by tablespoonfuls on baking sheets without grease, leaving 2inchspace apart. Bake until it turns lightly browned or for 16 to 18 minutes at 350 degrees. Allow to cool by moving to wire racks. Keep in an airtight container.

Nutrition Information: Calories: 117 calories Total Carbohydrate: 16 g Cholesterol: 16 mg Total Fat: 5 g Fiber: 1 g Protein: 2 g Sodium: 59 mg

Midnight Moon Pies

Serving: 2 dozen. | Prep: 20m | Ready in: 30m

Ingredients

- 2/3 cup dark chocolate chips
- 1/2 cup butter, cubed
- 2 cups all-purpose flour
- 2/3 cup sugar
- 1/3 cup packed brown sugar
- 1/4 cup baking cocoa
- 1/2 tsp. baking soda
- 1/4 tsp. salt
- 1 egg, beaten
- 1/2 cup buttermilk
- 1 tsp. vanilla extract
- 1/4 tsp. almond extract
- FILLING:
- 2/3 cup dark chocolate chips
- 1/4 cup butter, cubed
- 4 oz. cream cheese, softened
- 1 jar (7 oz.) marshmallow creme
- 1/4 tsp. almond extract
- 1 cup miniature semisweet chocolate chips

Direction

1. Melt butter and chocolate chips in microwave; mix till smooth then cool.
2. Mix salt, baking soda, cocoa, sugars and flour in big bowl. Mix cooled chocolate mixture, extracts, buttermilk and egg; add to dry ingredients. Beat till batter is just moist, it will be very thick.

3. Drop with small scoop/ by tablespoonfuls on parchment paper-lined baking sheets, 2-in. apart.
4. Bake for 8-10 minutes till edges set at 350°; cool for 2 minutes. Transfer from pans onto wire racks; completely cool.
5. Filling: Melt butter and chocolate chips; mix till smooth. Cool. Beat almond extract, marshmallow crème and cream cheese till smooth in small bowl; beat cooled chocolate mixture in. Spread 1 heaping tsp. filling on bottoms of 1/2 of the cookies; top using leftover cookies.
6. In mini chocolate chips, roll sides of cookies; keep in the fridge.

Nutrition Information: Calories: 279 calories Total Carbohydrate: 37 g Cholesterol: 29 mg Total Fat: 14 g Fiber: 1 g Protein: 3 g Sodium: 122 mg

Cherry Shortbread Hearts

Serving: *about 1-1/2 dozen. | Prep: 20m | Ready in: 40m*

Ingredients

• 1-1/4 cups all-purpose flour
• 3 tbsps. sugar
• 1/2 cup cold butter, cubed
• 1/2 cup maraschino cherries, patted dry and finely chopped
• 1 tbsp. cold water
• 1/4 tsp. almond extract
• 1 cup (6 oz.) semisweet chocolate chips
• 1 tbsp. shortening

Direction

1. Mix sugar and flour in big bowl; cut butter in till crumbly. Mix extract, water and cherries in till dough becomes a ball.
2. Roll dough to 1/4-in. thick on lightly floured surface; use floured 2 1/2-in. heart-shaped cookie cutter to cut. Put on ungreased baking sheets, 1-in. apart.
3. Bake for 20-25 minutes till edges lightly brown at 325°. Put on wire racks; cool.
4. Melt shortening and chocolate chips in microwave; mix till smooth. Dip 1/2 of every cookie into chocolate; let excess drip off. Put on waxed paper till set.

Nutrition Information: Calories: 119 calories Total Carbohydrate: 14 g Cholesterol: 11 mg Total Fat: 7 g Fiber: 1 g Protein: 1 g Sodium: 46 mg

Cherry Whoopie Pies

Serving: *3 dozen. | Prep: 30m | Ready in: 40m*

Ingredients

• 1 package red velvet cake mix (regular size)
• 3 large eggs
• 1/2 cup canola oil

- 1 tsp. almond extract
- 36 maraschino cherries, halved
- FILLING:
- 3/4 cup canned cream cheese frosting
- 2/3 cup whipped topping
- 1/2 cup chopped maraschino cherries

Direction

1. Beat extract, oil, eggs and cake mix for 30 seconds on low speed in big bowl; beat for 2 minutes on medium.
2. By heaping teaspoonfuls, drop on greased baking sheets, 2-in. apart. Put cherry half over each; bake for 8-10 minutes at 350° till edges set. Cool for 2 minutes. Transfer to wire racks; completely cool.
3. Filling: Beat whipped topping and frosting till blended; fold chopped cherries in. Spread filling on bottoms of 1/2 cookies; put leftover cookies on top. Refrigerate till serving.

Nutrition Information: Calories: 138 calories Total Carbohydrate: 20 g Cholesterol: 18 mg Total Fat: 6 g Fiber: 0 g Protein: 1 g Sodium: 116 mg

Cherry-filled Heart Cookies

Serving: about 4-1/2 dozen filled cookies. | Prep: 50m | Ready in: 60m

Ingredients

- 1/2 cup butter, softened
- 1/2 cup shortening
- 1 cup sugar
- 1 large egg
- 1/2 cup milk
- 1 tsp. vanilla extract
- 3-1/2 cups all-purpose flour
- 2 tsps. baking powder
- 1 tsp. baking soda
- 1/2 tsp. salt
- FILLING:
- 1/2 cup sugar
- 4-1/2 tsps. cornstarch
- 1/2 cup orange juice
- 1/4 cup red maraschino cherry juice
- 12 red maraschino cherries, chopped
- 1 tbsp. butter
- Additional sugar

Direction

1. Cream shortening and butter in bowl; add sugar slowly. Add vanilla, milk and egg. Mix dry ingredients;

add to creamed mixture slowly. Stir well. Cover; refrigerate for a minimum of 2 hours.

2. Meanwhile, for filling, mix cornstarch and sugar in small saucepan. Put in butter, cherries, and juices; bring to a boil. Mix and boil for 1 minute then chill.

3. Roll dough out to 1/8-in. thick on lightly floured surface; use 2 1/2-in. heart-shaped cookie cutter that is dipped in flour to cut.

4. Put 1/2 of cookies on greased baking sheets; put 1/2 tsp. filling in middle of each. Cut small hearts out of the other 1/2 of cookies with a 1 1/2-in. heart-shaped cutter; separately bake small heart cutouts. Put leftover hearts on filled cookies; gently press edges together. If needed, use extra filling to fill middles. Sprinkle sugar over.

5. Bake for 8-10 minutes at 375° till lightly browned. On wire racks, cool.

Nutrition Information: Calories: 183 calories Total Carbohydrate: 26 g Cholesterol: 19 mg Total Fat: 8 g Fiber: 0 g Protein: 2 g Sodium: 164 mg

Chocolate Almond Drops

Serving: 4 dozen. | Prep: 20m | Ready in: 30m

Ingredients

• 2 cups (12 oz.) semisweet chocolate chips
• 1 can (14 oz.) sweetened condensed milk
• 1 cup granola without raisins
• 1/2 cup sliced almonds
• 3 cups (18 oz.) miniature semisweet chocolate chips

Direction

1. Melt milk and chocolate chips, occasionally mixing, in heavy saucepan on low heat. Take off heat; mix almonds and granola in. Refrigerate for 1 hour till firm enough to roll.

2. Form mixture to 1-in. balls; roll in mini chocolate chips. Refrigerate for 2 hours till firm, covered. Keep in the fridge.

Nutrition Information: Calories: 127 calories Total Carbohydrate: 18 g Cholesterol: 3 mg Total Fat: 7 g Fiber: 2 g Protein: 2 g Sodium: 13 mg

Chocolate Caramel Kiss Cookies

Serving: about 2 dozen. | Prep: 15m | Ready in: 25m

Ingredients

• 1/2 cup butter, softened
• 1/2 cup packed brown sugar
• 1 cup granulated sugar, divided
• 1 large egg plus 1 large egg yolk
• 1-1/2 tsps. vanilla extract
• 1-1/4 cups all-purpose flour

- 3/4 cup baking cocoa
- 1 tsp. baking soda
- 1 tsp. ground cinnamon
- 3/4 tsp. salt
- 24 caramel-filled milk chocolate kisses

Direction

1. Heat the oven beforehand to 350 degrees. Cream half cup of granulated sugar, brown sugar and butter until fluffy and light. Stir in vanilla, egg yolk and egg. Whisk the next 5 ingredients in a different bowl then beat into the creamed mixture gradually.
2. Form rounded tbsps. of dough into balls. Roll in the leftover sugar. Put on baking sheets without grease, leaving 2-inch space apart. Bake for 8 to 10 minutes until edges begin to turn brown. Press a chocolate kiss immediately in the middle of every cookie, crack will form around edges. Allow to cool on pans for 2 minutes. Allow to cool by moving to wire racks.

Nutrition Information: Calories: 143 calories Total Carbohydrate: 23 g Cholesterol: 27 mg Total Fat: 6 g Fiber: 1 g Protein: 2 g Sodium: 170 mg

Chocolate Cherry Cookies

Serving: 4 dozen. | Prep: 25m | Ready in: 35m

Ingredients

- 1/2 cup butter, softened
- 1 cup sugar
- 1 egg
- 2 tsps. maraschino cherry juice
- 1-1/2 tsps. vanilla extract
- 1-1/2 cups all-purpose flour
- 1/2 cup baking cocoa
- 1/4 tsp. salt
- 1/4 tsp. baking powder
- 1/4 tsp. baking soda
- 24 maraschino cherries, drained and halved
- FROSTING:
- 1 cup (6 oz.) semisweet chocolate chips
- 1/2 cup sweetened condensed milk
- 1 tsp. maraschino cherry juice

Direction

1. Cream sugar and butter in big bowl; beat vanilla, cherry juice and egg in. Mix baking soda, baking powder, salt, cocoa and flour; add to creamed mixture slowly.
2. Roll to 1-in. balls; put on ungreased baking sheets, 2-in. apart. Make indentation in middle of each with the end of a wooden spoon. Put a cherry half in every indentation.

3. Melt milk and chocolate chips, constantly mixing, in small saucepan on low heat. Take off heat; mix cherry juice in till blended. Put 1 tsp. on each cherry, the frosting will spread on cookies while baking. Bake for 9-11 minutes at 350° till set. Transfer to wire racks; cool.

Nutrition Information: Calories: 167 calories Total Carbohydrate: 26 g Cholesterol: 21 mg Total Fat: 7 g Fiber: 1 g Protein: 2 g Sodium: 92 mg

Chocolate Chip Meringue Cookies

Serving: 20 | Prep: 25m | Ready in: 55m

Ingredients

- 2/3 cup granulated sugar
- 2 tsps. cornstarch
- 3 egg whites, at room temperature
- 1/2 tsp. white vinegar
- 1/2 cup mini semi-sweet chocolate chips
- 3 tbsps. unsweetened cocoa powder
- Garnish:
- Cocoa powder (optional)

Direction

1. Heat the oven beforehand to 150°C or 300°F. Use parchment paper to line 2 big baking sheets.
2. Whisk cornstarch and sugar together in a small bowl then leave aside.
3. Use an electric mixer to beat egg whites until foamy in a big bowl. Beat in vinegar until get soft peaks formed for about 2 minutes on medium speed. Beat in sugar mixture until get stiff glossy peaks formed on high speed, putting 15ml or 1 tbsp. at a time for about 2 to 3 minutes. Fold in cocoa powder and chocolate chips until just combined.
4. By tablespoonfuls, drop about 15ml on baking sheets that were prepared, leaving about 5cm or 1-inch space apart. Bake until cookies are dry to touch while rotating the pans halfway through or for 30 minutes. Transfer cookies onto cooling racks from sheets. If desired, sprinkle cocoa powder. Allow to cool completely; keep in airtight containers.

Nutrition Information: Calories: 52 calories; Total Carbohydrate: 2 g Cholesterol: 0 mg Total Fat: 4 g Protein: 9 g Sodium: 9 mg

Chocolate Chip Red Velvet Whoopie Pies

Serving: about 2 dozen. | Prep: 45m | Ready in: 55m

Ingredients

- 1 package red velvet cake mix (regular size)
- 3 large eggs
- 1/2 cup canola oil
- 2 tsps. vanilla extract

- FILLING:
- 8 oz. cream cheese, softened
- 1/2 cup butter, softened
- 2 cups confectioners' sugar
- 1 cup (6 oz.) miniature semisweet chocolate chips

Direction

1. Preheat an oven to 350°. Beat extract, oil, eggs and cake mix for 30 seconds on low speed in big bowl; beat for 2 minutes on medium.
2. Cut 1/2-in. hole in tip of pastry bag/in corner of food-safe plastic bag; put dough in bag. On parchment paper-lined baking sheets, pipe 1 1/2 x1-in. hearts; space hearts an inch apart.
3. Bake till edges set, about 6-8 minutes; cool for 2 minutes on pan. Transfer to wire racks; completely cool.
4. Filling: Beat butter and cream cheese till blended in big bowl; beat confectioners' sugar in slowly till smooth. Mix chocolate chips in; on bottom of 1/2 of cookies, spread filling. Top with leftover cookies then refrigerate leftovers.

Nutrition Information: Calories: 267 calories Total Carbohydrate: 30 g Cholesterol: 44 mg Total Fat: 16 g Fiber: 1 g Protein: 2 g Sodium: 194 mg

Chocolate Hazelnut Shortbread

Serving: *about 7-1/2 dozen. | Prep: 30m | Ready in: 40m*

Ingredients

- 1 cup butter, softened
- 1/3 cup Nutella
- 1 cup confectioners' sugar
- 1 large egg
- 3-3/4 cups all-purpose flour
- 1 tsp. ground cinnamon
- Dash salt
- 1/2 cup finely chopped hazelnuts
- Additional confectioners' sugar, optional

Direction

1. Heat the oven beforehand to 350 degrees. Cream confectioners' sugar, Nutella and butter until fluffy and light then stir in egg. Whisk salt, cinnamon and flour in a different bowl; mix in the creamed mixture gradually. Put hazelnuts and stir well.
2. Cut the dough into 2 parts and form into disk. Make 1/8-inch thickness dough by rolling on a lightly floured surface. Cut the dough using 2 1/4-inch scalloped round cookie cutter with flour; put on baking sheets without grease, leaving 1-inch space apart. Bake for 8 to 10 minutes until bottoms turn light brown. Allow to cool by putting transferring to wire racks from pans. Dust confectioners' sugar if desired.

Nutrition Information: Calories: 51 calories Total Carbohydrate: 6 g Cholesterol: 7 mg Total Fat: 3 g Fiber: 0 g Protein: 1 g Sodium: 33 mg

Chocolate Heart Cookies

Serving: about 2 dozen. | Prep: 30m | Ready in: 40m

Ingredients

- 1 cup butter, softened
- 1/2 cup sugar
- 1 tsp. vanilla extract
- 2 cups all-purpose flour
- 1/4 cup baking cocoa
- 1 cup vanilla or white chips
- 2 tbsps. shortening, divided
- 1/2 cup semisweet chocolate chips

Direction

1. Cream sugar and butter till fluffy and light in small bowl; beat vanilla in. Mix cocoa and flour; add to creamed mixture slowly. Stir well.
2. Roll dough out to 1/4-in. thick on lightly floured surface; use 3-in. heart-shaped cookie cutter to cut. Put on ungreased baking sheets, 2-in. apart.
3. Bake for 8-10 minutes till firm at 375°. Transfer to wire racks; cool.
4. Melt 1 tbsp. shortening and vanilla chips for 1 minute at 70% powder in microwave; mix. Microwave at extra 10- to 20-second intervals, mixing till smooth.
5. Dip both cookies' sides in melted mixture; let excess drip off. Put on waxed paper; stand till set.
6. Melt leftover shortening and chocolate chips in microwave; mix till smooth. Drizzle on cookies; put on wire racks to dry.

Nutrition Information: Calories: 188 calories Total Carbohydrate: 19 g Cholesterol: 22 mg Total Fat: 12 g Fiber: 1 g Protein: 2 g Sodium: 84 mg

Chocolate Linzer Torte Stars

Serving: about 1-1/2 dozen. | Prep: 15m | Ready in: 20m

Ingredients

- 1 package (17-1/2 oz.) sugar cookie mix
- 1/3 cup ground hazelnuts
- 1/4 cup all-purpose flour
- 2 tbsps. baking cocoa
- 1/2 tsp. ground cinnamon
- 1/8 tsp. ground cloves
- 1/2 cup butter, melted

- 1 large egg
- 1/2 tsp. vanilla extract
- 1/2 cup seedless raspberry preserves
- 4 oz. white baking chocolate, melted

Direction

1. Prepare the oven by preheating to 375°F. Mix the first six ingredients. Mix in vanilla, egg, and butter until combined.
2. Roll dough on a lightly floured surface to 1/4-inch thickness. Use a floured 2-1/2-inch star-shaped cookie cutter to cut. Set 1-inch apart on baking sheets that are not greased. Place in the preheated oven and bake for 5-7 minutes until set. Let cool for 2 minutes on pans. Take to wire racks to fully cool.
3. Place preserves on bottoms and half of the cookies then spread; then remaining cookies to cover. Dot with dissolved chocolate. Allow standing until set.

Nutrition Information: Calories: 238 calories Total Carbohydrate: 33 g Cholesterol: 24 mg Total Fat: 11 g Fiber: 0 g Protein: 2 g Sodium: 113 mg

Chocolate Marshmallow Meltaways

Serving: *3 dozen. | Prep: 20m | Ready in: 30m*

Ingredients

- 1/2 cup butter-flavored shortening
- 3/4 cup sugar
- 1 egg
- 1/4 cup 2% milk
- 1 tsp. vanilla extract
- 1-3/4 cups all-purpose flour
- 1/2 cup baking cocoa
- 1/2 tsp. salt
- 1/2 tsp. baking soda
- 18 large marshmallows, halved
- FROSTING:
- 3 tbsps. butter, softened
- 3 cups confectioners' sugar
- 3 tbsps. baking cocoa
- 1/8 tsp. salt
- 4 to 6 tbsps. 2% milk

Direction

1. Cream sugar and shortening in a large bowl until fluffy and light. Mix in vanilla, milk and egg. Mix the baking soda, salt, cocoa and flour; gently add to the creamed mixture and combine well.
2. Into ungreased baking sheets, drop by tablespoonfuls 2-inch apart. Place in the oven and bake for 8 minutes at 350°F. Press down a marshmallow half, cut side down, onto each cookie; bake for 2 more

minutes. Take out to wire racks to cool.

3. Beat salt, cocoa, confectioner's sugar and butter in a small bowl until smooth. Mix in enough milk to reach a spreading consistency. Then frost cookies.

Nutrition Information: Calories: 261 calories Total Carbohydrate: 46 g Cholesterol: 18 mg Total Fat: 8 g Fiber: 1 g Protein: 3 g Sodium: 147 mg

Chocolate Peanut Butter Thumbprints

Serving: about 3 dozen. | Prep: 35m | Ready in: 50m

Ingredients

• 1 cup butter-flavored shortening
• 1 cup sugar
• 2 egg yolks
• 2 tbsps. milk
• 2 oz. unsweetened chocolate, melted and cooled
• 1 tsp. vanilla extract
• 2 cups all-purpose flour
• 1/2 tsp. salt
• 2/3 cup miniature semisweet chocolate chips
• FILLING:
• 1/3 cup creamy peanut butter
• 2 tbsps. butter-flavored shortening
• 1 cup plus 2 tbsps. confectioners' sugar
• 2 tbsps. milk
• 1/2 tsp. vanilla extract

Direction

1. Cream sugar and shortening in big bowl; beat vanilla, melted chocolate, milk and egg yolks in. Mix salt and flour; add to chocolate mixture slowly. Mix chocolate chips in; roll to 1-in. balls.
2. Put on greased baking sheets, 2-in. apart. Make an indentation in middle of every ball with the end of wooden spoon handle; bake for 11-13 minutes at 350° till firm. Transfer to wire racks; completely cool.
3. Meanwhile, for filling: Beat shortening and peanut butter till combined in small bowl; beat vanilla, milk and confectioners' sugar in till smooth. Use filling to fill cookies; keep in airtight container.

Nutrition Information: Calories: 135 calories Total Carbohydrate: 15 g Cholesterol: 10 mg Total Fat: 8 g Fiber: 0 g Protein: 1 g Sodium: 41 mg

Chocolate Peppermint Spritz Cookies

Serving: 3 dozen. | Prep: 25m | Ready in: 35m

Ingredients

• 3/4 cup butter, softened

- 3/4 cup sugar
- 1 large egg
- 1-1/2 tsps. peppermint extract
- 1 tsp. vanilla extract
- 1-1/2 cups all-purpose flour
- 1/4 cup baking cocoa
- 1/8 tsp. salt
- 1/4 cup crushed peppermint candies

Direction

1. Heat the oven beforehand to 375 degrees. Cream the sugar and butter until fluffy and light in a big bowl. Mix extracts and egg in. Whisk salt, cocoa and flour in a different bowl; mix in the creamed mixture gradually.
2. Press the dough onto baking sheets without grease using a cookie press fitted with a disk of your choice, leaving 1-inch space apart. Bake until set or for 8 to 12 minutes. Sprinkle crushed candies immediately on top of cookies. Allow to cool completely by transferring to wire racks from pans. Keep in airtight containers.

Nutrition Information: Calories: 76 calories Total Carbohydrate: 9 g Cholesterol: 15 mg Total Fat: 4 g Fiber: 0 g Protein: 1 g Sodium: 41 mg

Chocolate Sugar Cookies

Serving: 18

Ingredients

- 3/4 cup shortening
- 1 cup white sugar
- 1 egg
- 1/4 cup light corn syrup
- 2 (1 oz.) squares unsweetened chocolate, melted
- 2 cups all-purpose flour
- 1/4 tsp. salt
- 1 tsp. baking soda
- 1 tsp. ground cinnamon

Direction

1. Preheat an oven to 175°C/350°F.
2. Cream egg, sugar and shortening in big mixing bowl; mix melted chocolate and syrup in. Sift ground cinnamon, baking soda, salt and flour; add to creamed mixture then chill for an hour.
3. Roll dough on well-floured pastry cloth to 1/8-in. thick; cut to shapes.
4. Bake for 10-12 minutes on ungreased cookie sheet.

Nutrition Information: Calories: 202 calories; Total Carbohydrate: 3 g Cholesterol: 10 mg Total Fat: 6 g Protein: 2 g Sodium: 110 mg

Chocolate-cherry Sandwich Cookies

Serving: 3-1/2 dozen. | Prep: 35m | Ready in: 35m

Ingredients

• 4 oz. cream cheese, softened
• 1/2 cup confectioners' sugar
• 1/2 cup finely chopped maraschino cherries, drained
• 1/4 tsp. almond extract
• 1 package (12 oz.) vanilla wafers
• 18 oz. milk chocolate candy coating, melted
• Red nonpareils or red colored sugar

Direction

1. Beat confectioners' sugar and cream cheese until it becomes smooth in a small bowl. Mix in extract and cherries. Spread a tsp. of cream cheese mixture on half of the wafers' bottoms. Use leftover wafers to cover. Put in the refrigerator until filling is firm or for an hour.
2. Immerse the sandwiches in the candy coating. Let the excess drip off the sandwich. Put on waxed paper and use nonpareils to sprinkle. Let rest until set. Keep in the refrigerator in an airtight container.

Chocolate-cherry Thumbprint Cookies

Serving: 2-1/2 dozen. | Prep: 50m | Ready in: 60m

Ingredients

• 3/4 cup butter, softened
• 1/2 cup sugar
• 1 large egg yolk
• 1 tsp. vanilla extract
• 1-1/2 cups all-purpose flour
• 1/4 cup baking cocoa
• FILLING:
• 1 cup confectioners' sugar
• 1/4 cup butter, softened
• 1 tbsp. maraschino cherry juice
• TOPPING:
• 30 maraschino cherries, patted dry
• 1/4 cup semisweet chocolate chips
• 1-1/2 tsps. shortening

Direction

1. Heat the oven beforehand to 350 degrees. Cream the sugar and butter until fluffy and light in a big bowl.

Beat in vanilla and egg yolk. Whisk cocoa and flour in a separate bowl then beat into the creamed mixture gradually.

2. Form into 1-inch balls then put them on baking sheets with grease, leaving 2-inch space apart. Use the end of a wooden spoon handle to press a deep indentation in the middle of each of the dough. Bake until firm or for 7 to 9 minutes. Allow it to cool by putting it on wire racks.
3. Make the filling by beating cherry juice, butter and confectioners' sugar in a small bowl. Put 1/2 tsp. of filling in each cookie and put cherry on top. Melt shortening and chocolate chips in a microwave. Mix until it becomes smooth; drizzle on top of cookies. Let rest until set.

Nutrition Information: Calories: 84 calories Total Carbohydrate: 11 g Cholesterol: 14 mg Total Fat: 4 g Fiber: 0 g Protein: 1 g Sodium: 27 mg

Chocolate-covered Maraschino Cherry Cookies

Serving: 2 dozen. | Prep: 45m | Ready in: 60m

Ingredients

• 24 maraschino cherries
• 1/2 cup butter, softened
• 3/4 cup packed brown sugar
• 1 tbsp. maraschino cherry juice
• 1 tsp. vanilla extract
• 1-1/2 cups all-purpose flour
• 1/8 tsp. salt
• 1 cup milk chocolate chips, divided
• 1/2 tsp. shortening

Direction

1. Use paper towels to pat cherries to remove extra moisture; put aside. Cream brown sugar and butter till fluffy and light in big bowl; beat vanilla and cherry juice in. Mix salt and flour; add to creamed mixture slowly. Stir well. Cover; refrigerate till dough is easy to handle, about 1 hour.
2. Put a chocolate chip into every maraschino cherry; wrap 1 tbsp. dough around every cherry. Put on ungreased baking sheets, 1-in. apart.
3. Bake for 15-17 minutes till set and edges lightly brown at 350°; transfer to wire racks then cool.
4. Melt shortening and leftover chips in microwave; mix till smooth. Dip cookies' tops in melted chocolate; let excess drip off. Put on waxed paper; stand till set. Keep in airtight container.

Cocoa Brownie Cookies

Serving: 16 cookies. | Prep: 15m | Ready in: 25m

Ingredients

- 1/2 cup butter, softened
- 1 cup packed brown sugar
- 3 large eggs
- 8 oz. semisweet chocolate, melted and slightly cooled
- 1 tsp. vanilla extract
- 1-1/4 cups all-purpose flour
- 1/4 cup baking cocoa
- 1/2 tsp. baking powder
- Dash salt
- 1 cup semisweet chocolate chunks

Direction

1. Preheat an oven to 350°. Cream brown sugar and butter till fluffy and light in big bowl; one by one, beat eggs in, beating well with every addition. Beat vanilla and chocolate in. Whisk salt, baking powder, cocoa and flour in small bowl; mix into creamed mixture. Fold chocolate chunks in.
2. By 1/4 cupfuls, drop dough on lightly greased baking sheets, 3-in. apart. Spread each to 3-in. diameter then bake till cookies are just set and tops are cracked, about 9-11 minutes. Cool for 2 minutes on pans; transfer to wire racks then cool.

Coconut-macadamia Biscotti

Serving: about 2-1/2 dozen. | Prep: 20m | Ready in: 01h15m

Ingredients

- 6 tbsps. butter, softened
- 3/4 cup sugar
- 1/3 cup canola oil
- 3 large eggs
- 2 tsps. vanilla extract
- 1 tsp. coconut extract
- 3-1/4 cups all-purpose flour
- 1-3/4 tsps. baking powder
- 1/4 tsp. salt
- 1 cup sweetened shredded coconut, toasted and finely chopped
- 1 cup macadamia nuts, coarsely chopped
- 2 cups (12 oz.) semisweet chocolate chips
- 2 tbsps. shortening

Direction

1. Heat the oven beforehand to 350 degrees. Beat oil, sugar and butter until blended in a big bowl. Beat in extracts and eggs. Whisk salt, baking powder and flour in a different bowl; mix in the creamed mixture gradually. Mix in nuts and coconut.
2. Divide the dough into Shape each part into 8x3-inch rectangle on baking sheets lined with parchment

paper. Bake until set for about 25 minutes.

3. Transfer pans onto wire racks; put baked rectangles into cutting board once cool enough to handle. Slice crosswise into half inch slices using a serrated knife. Put back to pans with the cut side down.
4. Bake until golden brown or for 15 to 18 minutes on each side. Allow to cool completely by transferring to wire racks from pans.
5. Melt shortening and chocolate chips in a microwave then mix until smooth. Dunk each cookie in the mixture halfway through; let the excess drip. Put on waxed paper until set then keep in an airtight container.

Colorful Peanut Butter Crackers

Serving: 2 dozen. | Prep: 35m | Ready in: 35m

Ingredients

- 4 oz. cream cheese, cubed
- 1/2 cup creamy peanut butter
- 1/4 cup honey
- 48 butter-flavored crackers
- 2 cups (12 oz.) semisweet chocolate chips
- 4 tsps. shortening
- 1/4 cup 2% milk
- Cake decorator holiday shapes

Direction

1. Heat cream cheese on high till very soft in microwave-safe bowl, about 15 seconds. Add honey and peanut butter; mix till smooth. Spread on 1/2 of crackers; put leftover crackers on top.
2. Melt shortening and chocolate chips in microwave; mix till smooth. Heat milk; mix into chocolate mixture.
3. Dip every cracker sandwich in chocolate mixture; let excess drip off. Put on waxed paper-lined baking sheets; as desired, decorate. Refrigerate till set for 45 minutes.

Contest-winning Chocolate Mint Wafers

Serving: about 1-1/2 dozen. | Prep: 20m | Ready in: 20m

Ingredients

- 4 oz. dark chocolate candy coating
- 1/8 to 1/4 tsp. peppermint extract
- 18 to 24 vanilla wafers

Direction

1. Put the extract and candy coating in a microwave-safe bowl. Microwave until smooth or for 30 to 60

seconds, stirring after every 15 seconds without a cover on high.
2. Dunk the vanilla wafers in the coating then let the excess to dip off. Put on waxed paper then allow to rest until set. Keep in an airtight container.

Nutrition Information: Calories: 38 calories Total Carbohydrate: 5 g Cholesterol: 0 mg Total Fat: 2 g Fiber: 0 g Protein: 0 g Sodium: 9 mg

Cookie Pizza A La Mode

Serving: *6 servings. | Prep: 5m | Ready in: 20m*

Ingredients

• 1 tube (16-1/2 oz.) refrigerated chocolate chip cookie dough
• Chocolate syrup
• Vanilla ice cream
• 6 maraschino cherries, optional

Direction

1. Press cookie dough on ungreased 12-in. pizza pan; bake for 15-20 minutes till deep golden brown at 350°. Cool for 5 minutes on wire rack; cut to 6 wedges.
2. On dessert plates, drizzle chocolate syrup; top with extra chocolate syrup, ice cream and warm cookie wedges. If desired, garnish with a cherry.

Nutrition Information: Calories: 387 calories Total Carbohydrate: 55 g Cholesterol: 20 mg Total Fat: 17 g Fiber: 1 g Protein: 4 g Sodium: 178 mg

Cranberry Almond Biscotti

Serving: *15 | Prep: 30m | Ready in: 1h30m*

Ingredients

• 2 1/4 cups all-purpose flour
• 1 cup white sugar
• 1 tsp. baking powder
• 1/2 tsp. baking soda
• 2 egg whites
• 2 eggs
• 1 tbsp. vanilla extract
• 3/4 cup sliced almonds
• 1 cup sweetened-dried cranberries

Direction

1. Heat the oven beforehand to 170°C or 325°F.
2. In a medium sized mixing bowl, mix the dry ingredients. In another mixing bowl, whisk almond extract

or vanilla, egg whites and eggs together.

3. Pour egg mixture to the dry ingredients, stirring just till moist, with an electric mixer on medium speed. Put almonds and dried cranberries in then thoroughly mix.
4. Divide the batter into 2 parts on a floured surface then pat each part into a log with a size of approximately 1 1/2 inch thick and 14 inches long. Put on a cookie sheet. Bake until firm or for 30 minutes. Allow it to cool until cool enough to handle or for about 10 minutes by putting on a wire rack.
5. Slice the biscotti diagonally into half inch slices. Turn the temperature of the oven down to 150°C or 300°F. Put the sliced biscotti on a cookie sheet on an upright position, leaving about 1 inch space apart. Bake for another 20 minutes. Allow to cool and keep in a container with a loose cover.

Nutrition Information: Calories: 189 calories; Total Carbohydrate: 5 g Cholesterol: 25 mg Total Fat: 2 g Protein: 2 g Sodium: 92 mg

Double-dipped Shortbread Cookies

Serving: about 2-1/2 dozen. | Prep: 15m | Ready in: 25m

Ingredients

- 3/4 cup butter, softened
- 1-1/2 cups confectioners' sugar
- 3 oz. semisweet chocolate, melted and cooled
- 1 tsp. vanilla extract
- 1-1/2 cups all-purpose flour
- 2 tsps. baking cocoa
- 1/8 tsp. salt
- 3 oz. semisweet chocolate, chopped
- 1/4 cup heavy whipping cream
- 4 oz. white baking chocolate, chopped

Direction

1. Cream the confectioners' sugar and butter until fluffy and light. Stir in vanilla and melted chocolate. Whisk salt, cocoa and flour in a different bowl then put in the creamed mixture gradually. Form rounded tbsps. of dough to 2-inch-long logs. Put in baking sheets without grease, leaving 2-inch space apart. Store in the refrigerator with cover for an hour.
2. Heat the oven beforehand to 350 degrees. Bake cookies for 8 to 10 minutes until edges are set. Allow to cool for 2 minutes on pans. Let to cool completely by putting on wire racks.
3. Melt semisweet chocolate with cream in a microwave and mix until smooth. Dip each cookie in the chocolate halfway through. Let the excess drip off then put on waxed paper. Melt white chocolate in the microwave then stir until smooth. Drizzle melted white chocolate on cookies and let rest until set.

Nutrition Information: Calories: 137 calories Total Carbohydrate: 14 g Cholesterol: 14 mg Total Fat: 8 g Fiber: 0 g Protein: 1 g Sodium: 47 mg

Dried Cherry Biscotti

Serving: 2-1/2 dozen. | Prep: 25m | Ready in: 50m

Ingredients

- 2 tbsps. butter, softened
- 1/2 cup sugar
- 4 egg whites
- 2 tsps. almond extract
- 2 cups all-purpose flour
- 2 tsps. baking powder
- 1/4 tsp. salt
- 1/2 cup dried cherries
- 1/4 cup chopped almonds, toasted
- 2 tsps. confectioners' sugar

Direction

1. Beat sugar and butter till crumbly in small bowl; beat extract and egg whites in. Mix salt, baking powder and flour; add to sugar mixture slowly. Mix almonds and cherries in; it will be stiff.
2. Press in 8-in. square baking dish coated in cooking spray. Bake for 15-20 minutes till lightly browned at 375°; cool for 5 minutes. Transfer from pan onto cutting board. Use a serrated knife to cut biscotti in half. Cut every half to 1/2-in. slices.
3. Put slices on baking sheets coated in cooking spray, cut side down. Bake till light golden brown, 8-10 minutes, turning once. Transfer to wire racks; cool. Sprinkle confectioners' sugar over.

Nutrition Information: Calories: 135 calories Total Carbohydrate: 24 g Cholesterol: 4 mg Total Fat: 3 g Fiber: 1 g Protein: 3 g Sodium: 123 mg

Easy Cinnamon Thins

Serving: 2-1/2 dozen. | Prep: 15m | Ready in: 20m

Ingredients

- 12 oz. white candy coating, chopped
- 1 tsp. cinnamon extract
- 30 Ritz crackers
- 12 finely crushed cinnamon hard candies
- Red colored sugar

Direction

1. Melt candy coating in a microwave and stir until smooth. Mix in extract.
2. Dunk the crackers in the candy coating mixture then let the excess drip off. Put on waxed paper and if desired, decorate using colored sugar and candies. Allow to rest until set.

Nutrition Information: Calories: 75 calories Total Carbohydrate: 10 g Cholesterol: 0 mg Total Fat: 4 g Fiber: 0 g Protein: 0 g Sodium: 36 mg

Engaging Heart Cookies

Serving: about 3-1/2 dozen. | Prep: 25m | Ready in: 35m

Ingredients

- 1 cup butter, softened
- 1/2 cup sugar
- 1/2 cup packed brown sugar
- 2 eggs
- 1 tsp. vanilla extract
- 2-1/4 cups all-purpose flour
- 1/4 cup baking cocoa
- 1/4 tsp. salt
- 3/4 cup ground toasted hazelnuts
- 3/4 cup semisweet chocolate chips
- 2 tbsps. shortening, divided
- 3/4 cup vanilla or white chips

Direction

1. Beat sugars and cream butter in a bowl. Mix in vanilla and eggs. Mix the salt, cocoa, and flour; stir to creamed mixture. Mix in hazelnuts. Split dough in half. Keep in the refrigerator for 1 hour, covered, or until easy to handle. Moving with one portion of dough at a time, turn to 1/4-inch thickness on a surface that is lightly floured. Use a 2-inch heart-shaped cookie cutter to cut. Set 1-inch apart on baking sheets that are not greased. Place in the oven and bake for 9-10 minutes at 350°F (cookies will be soft). Let cool for 1 minute prior taking to wire racks. Dissolve 1 tbsp. shortening and chocolate chips in a microwave-safe bowl; mix until smooth. Continue with remaining shortening and vanilla chips. Dunk right side of half of the cookies in semisweet chocolate; sink the left side of the remaining cookie in white chocolate. Extending two hearts before the chocolate is set. Put on waxed paper until set.

Nutrition Information: Calories: 263 calories Total Carbohydrate: 29 g Cholesterol: 45 mg Total Fat: 16 g Fiber: 1 g Protein: 3 g Sodium: 131 mg

Frosted Cutout Sugar Cookies

Serving: 5 dozen. | Prep: 30m | Ready in: 40m

Ingredients

- 3 cups all-purpose flour
- 1 cup granulated sugar
- 1 tsp. baking soda
- 1/4 tsp. salt
- 1/2 cup shortening
- 1/2 cup cold butter
- 2 large eggs
- 1 tbsp. whole milk
- 1 tsp. vanilla extract

- FROSTING:
- 1/2 cup butter, softened
- 4 cups confectioners' sugar
- 1 tsp. vanilla extract
- 2 to 4 tbsps. half-and-half cream
- Food coloring, optional
- Colored sugar, optional
- Decorating candies, optional

Direction

1. Mix salt, baking soda, granulated sugar and flour; cut butter and shortening in till crumbly. Whisk vanilla, milk and eggs in another bowl; add to flour mixture. Stir well then divide dough to 3 balls. Cover; refrigerate for 2 hours till easy to handle.
2. Preheat an oven to 325°; take one dough portion out of the fridge at a time. Roll dough to 1/4-in. thick on lightly floured surface. Use floured 2-in. cookie cutter to cut; put on ungreased baking sheets, 1-in. apart. Repeat with leftover dough.
3. Bake for 8-10 minutes till edges lightly brown. Cool for 1 minute; transfer to wire racks. Completely cool.
4. Frosting: Cream vanilla, confectioners' sugar, butter and enough cream to get spreading consistency. Tint with food coloring if desired; frost cookies. If desired, decorate with candies and colored sugar.

Nutrition Information: Calories: 112 calories Total Carbohydrate: 16 g Cholesterol: 15 mg Total Fat: 5 g Fiber: 0 g Protein: 1 g Sodium: 58 mg

Frosted Maple Pyramids

Serving: about 1-1/2 dozen. | *Prep: 25m* | *Ready in: 35m*

Ingredients

- 1/2 cup shortening
- 1/3 cup packed brown sugar
- 1 large egg
- 1 tsp. vanilla extract
- 1/4 tsp. maple flavoring
- 1-1/4 cups all-purpose flour
- 1/4 tsp. salt
- 1/4 tsp. baking powder
- FROSTING:
- 1/2 cup butter, softened
- 1-1/2 cups confectioners' sugar
- 2 tsps. vanilla extract
- Halved red candied cherries, optional

Direction

1. Cream the brown sugar and shortening until fluffy and light. Mix in maple flavoring, vanilla and egg. Whisk baking powder, salt and flour then stir in the creamed mixture gradually. Put in the refrigerator with a cover for about 2 hours until easy to handle.
2. Heat the oven beforehand to 375 degrees. Make 1/8-inch thickness dough by rolling out on a lightly floured surface. Slice out 18 circles using 2-inch round cooking cutters with flour. Repeat with 1-inch and 1 1/2-inch round cookie cutters; put on baking sheets with grease, leaving 1-inch space apart. Bake for 7 to 9 minutes till light brown. Allow to cool by putting on wire racks.
3. In the meantime, cream the confectioners' sugar and butter until fluffy and light then stir in vanilla. Make a small hole in a corner of a food-safe plastic bag or in the tip of a pastry bag; put frosting inside the bag. Assemble the cookies by putting a 2-inch cookie on the waxed paper. On top of the cookie, pipe the frosting; put1 1/2-inch cookie over then pipe. Put 1-inch cookie on top; pipe. If preferred, put candied cherries over.

Nutrition Information: Calories: 194 calories Total Carbohydrate: 23 g Cholesterol: 24 mg Total Fat: 11 g Fiber: 0 g Protein: 1 g Sodium: 88 mg

Mini-chip Crescent Cookies

Serving: about 6 dozen. | Prep: 40m | Ready in: 50m

Ingredients

- 1 cup butter, softened
- 1 package (8 oz.) cream cheese, softened
- 2 cups sugar
- 1 large egg
- 1 tsp. vanilla extract
- 1/4 tsp. almond extract
- 1/4 tsp. coconut extract, optional
- 3-1/2 cups all-purpose flour
- 1 tsp. baking powder
- 1-1/2 cups miniature semisweet chocolate chips
- 2 cups (12 oz.) semisweet chocolate chips
- 2 tbsps. shortening
- Toasted sweetened shredded coconut, optional

Direction

1. Beat sugar, cream cheese and butter until blended in a big bowl. Stir in extracts and egg. Whisk baking powder and flour in a different bowl; mix in the creamed mixture gradually. Mix in miniature chocolate chips then put in the refrigerator with cover until firm enough to shape or for an hour.
2. Heat the oven beforehand to 375 degrees. Make crescent shapes by forming level tbsps. of dough; on baking sheets with grease, put 1-inch space apart. Bake until lightly browned or for 10 to 12 minutes. Allow to cool completely by transferring to wire racks from pans.
3. Melt shortening and 2 cups of chocolate chips in a microwave. Mix until smooth. Dunk each cookie in the chocolate mixture halfway through; let excess drop off. Put on baking sheets lined with waxed paper. Sprinkle coconut if desired; keep in the refrigerator until set or for 30 minutes.

Nutrition Information: Calories: 121 calories Total Carbohydrate: 16 g Cholesterol: 13 mg Total Fat: 7 g Fiber: 1 g Protein: 1 g Sodium: 39 mg

Olive Oil Cookies

Serving: about 2 dozen. | Prep: 15m | Ready in: 25m

Ingredients

- 3/4 cup sugar
- 1/2 cup olive oil
- 1 egg
- 1/4 cup honey
- 1/4 tsp. lemon extract
- 1 cup all-purpose flour
- 1 cup whole wheat flour
- 2 tbsps. minced fresh rosemary
- 2 tsps. grated lemon peel
- 1-1/2 tsps. baking soda
- 1/4 tsp. plus 2 tsps. sea salt, divided

Direction

1. Beat oil and sugar till blended in big bowl; beat egg in then lemon extract and honey. Mix 1/4 tsp. salt, lemon peel, baking soda, rosemary and flours; add to sugar mixture slowly. Mix till just combined.
2. Drop by tablespoonfuls on parchment paper-lined baking sheets, 2-in. apart. Sprinkle leftover sea salt on tops; bake for 9-12 minutes till lightly browned at 350°. Transfer to wire racks; keep in airtight container.

Nutrition Information: Calories: 114 calories Total Carbohydrate: 17 g Cholesterol: 9 mg Total Fat: 5 g Fiber: 1 g Protein: 2 g Sodium: 303 mg

Papa's Sugar Cookies

Serving: 8 dozen. | Prep: 20m | Ready in: 30m

Ingredients

- 1 cup butter, softened
- 1 cup canola oil
- 1 cup sugar
- 1 cup confectioners' sugar
- 2 large eggs
- 2 tbsps. butter flavoring
- 1 tbsp. grated orange zest
- 1 tbsp. vanilla extract
- 5-1/2 cups all-purpose flour
- 1/4 cup ground macadamia nuts

- 1-1/2 tsps. baking soda
- 1 tsp. salt
- 1 tsp. cream of tartar
- 1 tsp. ground cinnamon
- Additional granulated sugar

Direction

1. Beat sugars, oil and butter until blended well in a big bowl. Put eggs, 1 at a time, stirring well before putting the next. Mix in vanilla, orange zest and butter flavoring.
2. Mix cinnamon, cream of tartar, salt, baking soda, nuts and flour then put in the butter mixture gradually. Stir well. Cover and put in the refrigerator until easy to handle or for an hour.
3. Make 1-inch balls by rolling. Roll in additional sugar. Put on baking sheets without grease, leaving 2-inch space apart. Flatten the balls using glass dipped in additional sugar.
4. Bake until edges begin to turn brown or for 10 to 12 minutes at 350 degrees. Put on wire racks.

Nutrition Information: Calories: 82 calories Total Carbohydrate: 9 g Cholesterol: 9 mg Total Fat: 5 g Fiber: 0 g Protein: 1 g Sodium: 60 mg

Peanut Butter Cutout Cookies

Serving: About 4-1/2 dozen. | Prep: 30m | Ready in: 40m

Ingredients

- 1 cup creamy peanut butter
- 3/4 cup sugar
- 3/4 cup packed brown sugar
- 2 large eggs
- 1/3 cup 2% milk
- 1 tsp. vanilla extract
- 2-1/2 cups all-purpose flour
- 1/2 tsp. baking powder
- 1/2 tsp. baking soda
- Vanilla frosting
- Red food coloring
- Assorted colored sprinkles

Direction

1. Cream sugars and peanut butter for 4 minutes till fluffy and light in big bowl; beat vanilla, milk and eggs in. Mix baking soda, baking powder and flour; add to creamed mixture. Stir well. Cover; refrigerate till easy to handle, about 2 hours.
2. Roll dough out to 1/4-in. thick on lightly floured surface. Use 2-4-in. cookie cutters to cut; put on ungreased baking sheets, 2-in. apart.
3. Bake for 7-9 minutes till edges are browned at 375°. Cool for a minute; transfer from pans onto wire racks to completely cool. Frost cookies then decorate as desired.

Nutrition Information: Calories: 151 calories Total Carbohydrate: 22 g Cholesterol: 16 mg Total Fat: 5 g Fiber: 1 g Protein: 4 g Sodium: 84 mg

Pink Peppermint Cookies

Serving: 4 dozen. | Prep: 15m | Ready in: 20m

Ingredients

- 1 cup butter, softened, divided
- 1/2 cup sugar
- 1 egg
- 10 to 12 drops red food coloring
- 3/4 tsp. peppermint extract
- 2 cups all-purpose flour, divided
- 1/2 tsp. baking soda
- 1/4 tsp. cream of tartar
- 1/4 tsp. salt
- 1 tbsp. chocolate syrup

Direction

1. Cream sugar and 3/4 cup butter in bowl; beat peppermint extract, food coloring and egg in. Mix salt, cream of tartar, baking soda and 1 3/4 cups flour; add to cream mixture. Form to a ball; cover. Chill for 1-2 hours. Meanwhile, mix leftover flour and butter and chocolate syrup till well blended in bowl. Put into pastry bag with small round tip; form dough to 3/4-in. balls. Put on ungreased baking sheets then flatten to 1 1/2-in. circles. Over cookies, pipe chocolate mixture with simple holiday designs. Bake for 5-7 minutes at 375°. On wire racks, cool.

Nutrition Information: Calories: 127 calories Total Carbohydrate: 13 g Cholesterol: 29 mg Total Fat: 8 g Fiber: 0 g Protein: 1 g Sodium: 131 mg

Pistachio Chocolate Macarons

Serving: about 1-1/2 dozen. | Prep: 35m | Ready in: 45m

Ingredients

- 3 large egg whites
- 1-1/4 cups confectioners' sugar
- 3/4 cup pistachios
- Dash salt
- 1/4 cup granulated sugar
- CHOCOLATE FILLING:
- 4 oz. bittersweet chocolate, chopped
- 1/2 cup heavy whipping cream
- 2 tsps. corn syrup

• 1 tbsp. butter

Direction

1. Allow egg whites to rest for 30 minutes at room temperature. In a food processor, pulse pistachios and confectioners' sugar until powdery.
2. Heat the oven beforehand to 350 degrees. Put salt in the egg whites then beat until get soft peaks formed on medium speed. Put sugar in gradually, 1 tbsp. at a time. Stir on high until stiff peaks formed; fold in pistachio mixture.
3. Slice a mall hole in a corner of a food-safe plastic bag or in the tip of a pastry bag then insert a star tip. Put pistachio mixture in the bag then pipe 1-inch- diameter cookies on baking sheets lined with parchment paper, leaving 1-inch space apart. Bake for 10 to 12 minutes until firm to the touch and lightly browned. Allow to cool completely on pans on wire racks.
4. Put the chocolate in a small bowl. Let corn syrup and cream boil in a small saucepan then pour on chocolate. Whisk till smooth. Whisk in butter then allow to cool at room temperature, occasionally stirring, or for about 45 minutes until filling reaches a spreading consistency. Pour over the bottoms of half of the cookies then cover using the leftover cookies.

Nutrition Information: Calories: 160 calories Total Carbohydrate: 16 g Cholesterol: 10 mg Total Fat: 9 g Fiber: 1 g Protein: 3 g Sodium: 135 mg

Pistachio Pinwheels

Serving: 5 dozen. | *Prep: 40m* | *Ready in: 50m*

Ingredients

• 1/3 cup butter, softened
• 1/3 cup sugar blend
• 2 large egg whites
• 3 tbsps. canola oil
• 1/2 tsp. vanilla extract
• 2-3/4 cups cake flour
• 1 tsp. baking powder
• 1/4 tsp. salt
• Red paste food coloring
• 1/2 cup pistachios, finely chopped

Direction

1. Cream the sugar and butter until fluffy and light in a big bowl then beat the vanilla, oi and egg whites in. Mix baking powder, flour and salt then put it into the butter mixture gradually. Stir well.
2. Cut the dough into two parts. Put food coloring on one part. Cut plain and red doughs in half. Between 2 sheets of waxed paper, make an 8x6-inch rectangle by rolling out one part of the plain dough. Repeat with one part of the red dough. Take away the waxed paper then put the red on top of the plain dough.
3. Starting with the long side, tightly roll the dough up on jelly-roll style. Roll the log in the pistachios; use plastic to wrap. Repeat with the rest of the doughs. Put it in the refrigerator until it becomes firm or for 2

hours.

4. Remove the plastic cover of the logs then slice into 1/4 inch slices. Put on baking sheets without grease, 2 inches apart. Bake it until set or for 7 to 9mins. Transfer it to wire racks.

Nutrition Information: Calories: 49 calories Total Carbohydrate: 6 g Cholesterol: 3 mg Total Fat: 2 g Fiber: 0 g Protein: 1 g Sodium: 33 mg

Pistachio-mint Meringue Cookies

Serving: 10 dozen. | Prep: 15m | Ready in: 01h15m

Ingredients

- 4 egg whites
- 1 tsp. vanilla extract
- 1/4 tsp. cream of tartar
- 1/4 tsp. salt
- 3/4 cup sugar
- 1 package (10 to 12 oz.) white baking chips
- 1 cup chopped pistachios
- 1 cup finely crushed peppermint candies
- Additional chopped pistachios, optional

Direction

1. Put egg whites in big bowl; stand for 30 minutes at room temperature.
2. Preheat an oven to 225°. Add salt, cream of tartar and vanilla to egg whites; beat till foamy on medium speed. 1 tbsp. at a time, add sugar slowly, beating on high after every addition till sugar melts; beat till stiff glossy peaks form. Fold crushed candies, pistachios and baking chips in.
3. By rounded teaspoonfuls, drop on parchment paper-lined baking sheets, 1-in. apart. Sprinkle extra pistachios over if desired; bake till firm to touch, about 1-1 1/4 hours. Transfer to wire racks; completely cool. Keep in airtight containers.

Raspberry & Pink Peppercorn Meringues

Serving: 4 dozen. | Prep: 15m | Ready in: 35m

Ingredients

- 3 large egg whites
- 1/4 tsp. cream of tartar
- Pinch salt
- 3/4 cup sugar
- 1 tsp. raspberry extract
- 5 to 8 drops food coloring, optional
- 1/4 cup semisweet chocolate chips
- 1 tsp. shortening

• 2 tbsps. whole pink peppercorns, crushed

Direction

1. Put egg whites in big bow; stand for 30 minutes at room temperature. Add salt and cream of tartar; beat till soft peaks form on medium speed. 1 tbsp. at a time, add sugar slowly, beating on high till sugar melts and stiff glossy peaks form; if desired, beat food coloring and extract in.
2. Cut small hole in corner of plastic/pastry bag; insert big star tip. Use egg white mixture to fill bag; pipe 1 1/4-in. diameter cookies on parchment paper-lined baking sheets. Bake for 20-25 minutes till dry and set at 300°. Turn off oven; leave meringues for 1 hour in oven. Transfer onto wire racks.
3. Melt shortening and chocolate chips in microwave; mix till smooth. Drizzle on cookies; sprinkle peppercorns over. Keep in airtight container.

Nutrition Information: Calories: 19 calories Total Carbohydrate: 4 g Cholesterol: 0 mg Total Fat: 0 g Fiber: 0 g Protein: 0 g Sodium: 7 mg

Raspberry Almonettes

Serving: about 3-1/2 dozen. | Prep: 60m | Ready in: 01h15m

Ingredients

• 1 cup butter, softened
• 2 cups sugar
• 2 large eggs
• 1 cup canola oil
• 2 tbsps. almond extract
• 4-1/2 cups all-purpose flour
• 1 tsp. salt
• 1 tsp. baking powder
• 3/4 cup sliced almonds, finely chopped
• FILLING :
• 1 package (8 oz.) cream cheese, softened
• 1/2 cup confectioners' sugar
• 1 tbsp. almond extract
• 1/4 cup red raspberry preserves

Direction

1. Heat the oven beforehand to 350 degrees. Cream the sugar and butter until fluffy and light in a big bowl. Put eggs in, one at a time. Beat well before putting another. Beat in extract and oil gradually. Whisk baking powder, salt and flour in a different bowl. Stir into the creamed mixture gradually.
2. Form dough into 1-inch balls. Press one side of the dough in the chopped almonds. Put into baking sheets without grease, leaving 2-inch space apart, almond side up. Use the bottom of the glass to flatten the dough to 1/4-inch thickness.
3. Bake until its edges turn light brown or for 8 to 10 minutes. Allow to cool on pans for 5 minutes. Allow to completely cool by moving to wire racks.

4. Make the filling by beating extract, confectioners' sugar, and cream cheese in a small bowl until smooth. On half of the cookies' bottoms, put rounded teaspoonfuls of filling. Indent the middle part of each cookie then fill using 1/4 tsp. of preserves. Use the remaining cookies to cover and keep in the refrigerator in an airtight container.

Nutrition Information: Calories: 216 calories Total Carbohydrate: 23 g Cholesterol: 26 mg Total Fat: 13 g Fiber: 1 g Protein: 2 g Sodium: 125 mg

Raspberry Coconut Balls

Serving: about 4 dozen. | Prep: 30m | Ready in: 30m

Ingredients

- 1 package (12 oz.) vanilla wafers, crushed
- 3-1/3 cups sweetened shredded coconut, divided
- 1 can (14 oz.) sweetened condensed milk
- 3 tsps. raspberry extract
- 1 tsp. rum extract
- 1/4 cup pink sanding sugar

Direction

1. Mix 1 1/3 cups coconut and wafer crumbs; mix extracts and milk in. Mix leftover coconut and sugar in shallow bowl; form dough to 1-in. balls then roll in coconut mixture. In airtight containers, refrigerate.

Nutrition Information: Calories: 93 calories Total Carbohydrate: 13 g Cholesterol: 4 mg Total Fat: 4 g Fiber: 1 g Protein: 1 g Sodium: 52 mg

Raspberry Dreams

Serving: about 4-1/2 dozen. | Prep: 25m | Ready in: 35m

Ingredients

- 2 cups butter, softened
- 1 cup granulated sugar
- 4 large egg yolks
- 2 tsps. vanilla extract
- 1 drop lemon juice
- 5-1/3 cups all-purpose flour
- 1/4 tsp. salt
- FILLING:
- 1 jar (12 oz.) red raspberry preserves
- ICING:
- 1 cup confectioners' sugar
- 1 drop lemon juice
- 1 drop red food coloring, optional

• 1 to 2 tbsps. 2% milk

Direction

1. Cream sugar and butter till fluffy and light; one by one, add egg yolks, beating well with every addition. Beat lemon juice and vanilla in. Whisk salt and flour in another bowl; beat into creamed mixture slowly. Refrigerate for 1 hour till easy to handle.
2. Preheat an oven to 350°; divide dough to 3 portions. Roll every portion to 1/4-in. thick on lightly floured surface. Use floured 2-in. round cookie cutter to cut; put on ungreased baking sheets, 1-in. apart. Bake for 8-10 minutes till edges are very lightly browned. Transfer to wire racks; cool.
3. Filling: Spread raspberry preserves on bottom 1/2 of the cookies; use leftover cookies to cover.
4. Icing: Mix food coloring (optional), lemon juice, sugar and enough milk to get drizzling consistency then drizzle on cookies.

Nutrition Information: Calories: 149 calories Total Carbohydrate: 20 g Cholesterol: 32 mg Total Fat: 7 g Fiber: 0 g Protein: 2 g Sodium: 66 mg

Red Velvet Peppermint Thumbprints

Serving: about 4 dozen. | Prep: 30m | Ready in: 40m

Ingredients

• 1 cup butter, softened
• 1 cup sugar
• 1 large egg
• 4 tsps. red food coloring
• 1 tsp. peppermint extract
• 2-1/2 cups all-purpose flour
• 3 tbsps. baking cocoa
• 1 tsp. baking powder
• 1/4 tsp. salt
• 2 cups white baking chips
• 2 tsps. canola oil
• 1/4 cup crushed peppermint candies

Direction

1. Heat the oven beforehand to 350 degrees. Cream the sugar and butter until fluffy and light in a big bowl. Stir in extract, coloring and egg. Whisk salt, cocoa, baking powder and flour in a different bowl then stir gradually into the creamed mixture.
2. Form the dough into 1-inch balls. Put on baking sheets without grease, leaving 1-inch space apart. Make a deep indentation in the middle of each by pressing using the end of a wooden spoon handle.
3. Bake until set or for 9 to 11 minutes. Allow to cool completely by transferring from the pans to wire racks.
4. Melt baking chips with oil in a microwave then mix until smooth. Put a scant tsp. of filling using spoon in every cookie. Use the remaining mixture to drizzle on tops. With peppermint candies, sprinkle and let

rest until set.

Nutrition Information: Calories: 118 calories Total Carbohydrate: 14 g Cholesterol: 16 mg Total Fat: 7 g Fiber: 0 g Protein: 1 g Sodium: 63 mg

Red Velvet White Chip Cookies

Serving: about 3-1/2 dozen. | Prep: 25m | Ready in: 35m

Ingredients

- 1/2 cup butter, softened
- 1/2 cup granulated sugar
- 1/2 cup packed brown sugar
- 1 large egg
- 1 tbsp. 2% milk
- 2 tsps. red food coloring
- 1 tsp. vanilla extract
- 1-1/2 cups all-purpose flour
- 1/3 cup baking cocoa
- 1 tsp. baking soda
- 1/4 tsp. salt
- 3/4 cup white baking chips

Direction

1. Heat the oven beforehand to 375 degrees. Cream the sugars and butter until fluffy and light in a big bowl. Stir in vanilla, food coloring, milk and egg. Whisk salt, baking soda, cocoa and flour in a different bowl then beat in the creamed mixture gradually. Mix in the baking chips.
2. By tablespoonfuls, drop the dough on the baking sheets lined with parchment paper, leaving 2-inch space apart. Bake for 6 to 8 minutes until set. Allow to cool for 2 minutes on pans. Allow to cool by putting on wire racks. You may put the cookies in freezer containers as freeze option and thaw before using.

Nutrition Information: Calories: 75 calories Total Carbohydrate: 11 g Cholesterol: 11 mg Total Fat: 3 g Fiber: 0 g Protein: 1 g Sodium: 67 mg

Salted Cashew Oatmeal Cookies

Serving: 1 batch (about 4 cups mix). | Prep: 20m | Ready in: 30m

Ingredients

- 1 cup all-purpose flour
- 3/4 tsp. baking soda
- 3/4 tsp. ground cinnamon
- 1/2 cup packed light brown sugar
- 1/2 cup sugar

- 1-1/3 cups old-fashioned oats
- 1 cup salted whole cashews
- ADDITIONAL INGREDIENTS:
- 2/3 cup butter, softened
- 3/4 tsp. vanilla extract
- 1 large egg plus 1 large egg yolk

Direction

1. Mix cinnamon, baking soda and flour. In order listed, layer flour mixture, brown sugar, granulated sugar, oats and cashews in a 1-qt. glass jar. Cover and keep in a cool dry place up to 3 months.
2. For preparing cookies: Preheat the oven to 350°. Whisk vanilla extract and butter till fluffy and light. Mix in yolk and egg till well incorporated. Put in cookie mixture; combine thoroughly.
3. Drop by tablespoonfuls 1-1/2 in. apart on baking sheets lined with parchment. Bake for 10 to 12 minutes till browned lightly. Take out and transfer to wire racks to cool down. Keep in an airtight container.

Nutrition Information: Calories: 104 calories Total Carbohydrate: 12 g Cholesterol: 19 mg Total Fat: 6 g Fiber: 1 g Protein: 2 g Sodium: 73 mg

Scottie Cookies

Serving: 7 dozen. | Prep: 02h30m | Ready in: 02h40m

Ingredients

- 1/2 cup butter, softened
- 1/2 cup butter-flavored shortening
- 2 tbsps. cream cheese, softened
- 1 cup sugar
- 2 large eggs
- 1 tsp. vanilla extract
- 1 tsp. light corn syrup
- 4 cups cake flour
- 1 tsp. baking powder
- 1/2 tsp. salt
- FROSTING:
- 3 cups confectioners' sugar
- 3 tbsps. cream cheese, softened
- 4-1/2 tsps. light corn syrup
- 3 to 4 tbsps. 2% milk
- Black liquid food coloring
- ROYAL ICING:
- 4 cups confectioners' sugar
- 6 tbsps. warm water (110° to 115°)
- 3 tbsps. meringue powder
- Red and green paste food coloring
- Assorted sprinkles

Direction

1. Cream sugar, cream cheese, shortening and butter till fluffy and light in big bowl; beat corn syrup, eggs and vanilla in. Mix salt, baking powder and flour; add to creamed mixture slowly. Stir well.
2. Divide dough into thirds; form each to a ball. Flatten into a disk. Use plastic to wrap; refrigerate till easy to handle, about 2 hours.
3. Roll 1 dough portion to 1/4-in. thick on lightly floured surface; use floured 3-in. dog-shaped cookie cutter to cut. Put on parchment paper-lined baking sheets, 1-in. apart. Repeat with leftover dough.
4. Bake for 7-9 minutes at 375° till edges lightly brown. Transfer to wire racks; completely cool.
5. Frosting: Mix corn syrup, cream cheese and confectioners' sugar in big bowl; add enough milk to get thin spreading consistency. Halve; leave one half plain and tint leftover half with black food coloring.
6. Royal icing: Beat meringue powder, water and confectioners' sugar on low speed till just combined in big bowl; beat for 4-5 minutes on high till stiff peaks form. Halve; tint one portion green and the other red. Use damp cloth to keep unused icing covered always. As desired, decorate cookies with sprinkles, icing and frosting. Dry for a few hours till firm at room temperature. Keep in airtight container in the fridge.

Nutrition Information: Calories: 99 calories Total Carbohydrate: 18 g Cholesterol: 9 mg Total Fat: 3 g Fiber: 0 g Protein: 1 g Sodium: 35 mg

Secret Kiss Cookies

Serving: 2-1/2 dozen. | Prep: 25m | Ready in: 40m

Ingredients

- 1 cup butter, softened
- 1/2 cup sugar
- 1 tsp. vanilla extract
- 2 cups all-purpose flour
- 1 cup finely chopped walnuts
- 30 milk chocolate kisses
- 1-1/3 cups confectioners' sugar, divided
- 2 tbsps. baking cocoa

Direction

1. Cream vanilla, sugar and butter till fluffy and light in big bowl. Add flour slowly; mix well. Fold walnuts in; refrigerate dough till firm, about 2-3 hours.
2. Preheat an oven to 375°; form to 1-in. balls. Flatten balls; put chocolate kiss in middle of each then pinch dough together around the kiss. Put on ungreased baking sheets, 2-in. apart.
3. Bake till set yet not browned, about 12 minutes. Cool for 1 minute; transfer from pans onto wire racks.
4. Sift cocoa and 2/3 cup confectioners' sugar. Roll half in cocoa mixture then half in leftover confectioners' sugar while cookies are still warm; completely cool. Keep in airtight container.

Nutrition Information: Calories: 366 calories Total Carbohydrate: 40 g Cholesterol: 36 mg Total Fat: 22 g Fiber: 2 g Protein: 5 g Sodium: 136 mg

Shortbread Hearts

Serving: about 2 dozen. | Prep: 20m | Ready in: 35m

Ingredients

- 2 cups all-purpose flour
- 1/2 cup sugar
- Dash salt
- 1 cup cold butter, cubed
- 1 tbsp. cold water
- 1 tsp. almond extract
- 1/2 lb. dark chocolate candy coating, melted

Direction

1. Mix salt, sugar and flour in big bowl; cut butter in till it looks like coarse crumbs. Mix extract and water in till mixture becomes a ball.
2. Roll dough out to 1/4-in. thick on lightly floured surface; use lightly floured 2 1/2-in. cookie cutter to cut. Put on ungreased baking sheets, 1-in. apart. Cover; refrigerate for 30 minutes.
3. Bake for 13-16 minutes till edges are lightly browned at 325°. Cool for 2 minutes; remove to wire racks to completely cool. Dip 1 side of cookie in candy coating; let excess drip off. Put onto waxed paper; let stand till set.

Nutrition Information: Calories: 171 calories Total Carbohydrate: 19 g Cholesterol: 20 mg Total Fat: 10 g Fiber: 0 g Protein: 1 g Sodium: 83 mg

Soft Buttermilk Sugar Cookies

Serving: about 2-1/2 dozen. | Prep: 20m | Ready in: 30m

Ingredients

- 1/2 cup shortening
- 1-1/4 cups sugar, divided
- 2 eggs
- 2 tsps. vanilla extract
- 2 cups all-purpose flour
- 2 tsps. baking powder
- 1 tsp. salt
- 1/2 tsp. baking soda
- 1/2 cup buttermilk
- 1/4 tsp. ground cinnamon

Direction

1. Cream 1 cup of sugar and shortening until fluffy and light in a big bowl. Beat in vanilla and eggs. Mix

baking soda, salt, baking powder and flour then put in the creamed mixture with the buttermilk alternatively. Beat well before putting the next. The batter will be moist.

2. Combine the remaining sugar and cinnamon. By tablespoonfuls, drop the dough on baking sheets with grease. Use cinnamon-sugar to sprinkle over.

3. Bake until edges begin to brown or for 8 to 10 minutes at 375 degrees. Put into wire racks. Keep it in an airtight container.

Nutrition Information: Calories: 90 calories Total Carbohydrate: 14 g Cholesterol: 13 mg Total Fat: 3 g Fiber: 0 g Protein: 1 g Sodium: 123 mg

Soft Peppermint Spritz Cookies

Serving: about 10 dozen. | Prep: 30m | Ready in: 40m

Ingredients

- 1 cup unsalted butter, softened
- 3 oz. cream cheese, softened
- 1 cup granulated sugar
- 1 large egg yolk
- 1 tsp. vanilla extract
- 1/2 tsp. peppermint extract
- 1-1/2 cups all-purpose flour
- 1 cup cornstarch
- 1/2 tsp. salt
- Paste food coloring of your choice
- Colored sugar, optional

Direction

1. Heat the oven beforehand to 350 degrees. Beat sugar, cream cheese and butter until fluffy and light in a big bowl. Stir in extracts and egg yolk. Whisk salt, cornstarch and flour in a different bowl then stir in the creamed mixture gradually.

2. Cut the dough into 2 parts. Use food coloring to tint one part. Press the dough using a cookie press fitted with a disk of your choice on baking sheets without grease, leaving 1-inch space apart. Sprinkle colored sugar if desired.

3. Bake until the edges become light golden or for 10 to 12 minutes. Let cool for 5 minutes on pans. Allow to cool by putting on wire racks. You can put cookies in freezer containers as freeze option; thaw before serving.

Nutrition Information: Calories: 26 calories Total Carbohydrate: 2 g Cholesterol: 6 mg Total Fat: 2 g Fiber 0 g Protein: 0 g Sodium: 12 mg

Sour Cream Sugar Cookies

Serving: 6 | Prep: 15m | Ready in: 2h25m

Ingredients

- Cookies:
- 1 1/2 cups white sugar
- 1 cup butter, softened
- 3 eggs
- 1 cup sour cream
- 2 tsps. vanilla extract
- 3 1/2 cups all-purpose flour
- 2 tsps. baking powder
- 1 tsp. baking soda
- Frosting:
- 1/3 cup butter, softened
- 2 cups confectioners' sugar
- 2 tbsps. milk, or more as needed
- 1 1/2 tsps. vanilla extract
- 1/4 tsp. salt

Direction

1. Use an electric mixer to beat 1 cup of butter and white sugar together until creamy in a big bowl. Put eggs in, one at a time. Stir well before putting the next. Stir 2 tsps. of vanilla extract and sour cream in the butter mixture.
2. In a bowl, mix baking soda, baking powder and flour together. Put flour mixture in the sour cream mixture. Mix well then use plastic wrap to cover the bowl. Put in the refrigerator for a minimum of 2 hours or overnight.
3. Heat the oven beforehand to 175°C or 350°F. Grease two baking sheets lightly.
4. Make 1/4-inch thick cookie by rolling the cookie dough on a floured surface. Slice into 3 inches round cookies. Put them on baking sheets that were prepared.
5. Bake for 10 to 12 minutes until cookies spring back when lightly touched in the middle in the preheated oven. Allow to cool completely by putting on wire racks.
6. Stir salt, 1 1/2 tsps. of vanilla extract, milk, confectioners' sugar and 1/3 cup of butter together until smooth in a bowl. Spread the frosting on top of the cooled cookies.

Nutrition Information: Calories: 1105 calories; Total Carbohydrate: 3 g Cholesterol: 219 mg Total Fat: 3 g Protein: 5 g Sodium: 819 mg

Special Chocolate Chip Cookies

Serving: about 4-1/2 dozen. | Prep: 60m | Ready in: 01h30m

Ingredients

- 1/2 cup quick-cooking oats
- 1 Nestlé Crunch candy bar (4 oz.), broken into pieces
- 1/4 cup chopped pecans
- 1 cup butter, softened
- 3/4 cup packed brown sugar
- 1/2 cup sugar

- 2 eggs
- 3 tsps. vanilla extract
- 2 cups all-purpose flour
- 1 tsp. baking soda
- 1/2 tsp. salt
- 1 cup semisweet chocolate chips
- 1 cup vanilla or white chips
- ICING:
- 2 cups confectioners' sugar
- 2 tbsps. milk
- 2 tsps. strawberry or raspberry extract
- 1 to 2 drops red food coloring, optional

Direction

1. Mix pecans, candy bat and oats in a food processor. Cover and process until chopped finely then set aside.
2. Cream the sugars and butter until fluffy and light in a big bowl. Put in eggs, one at a time. Beat well after every addition. Stir the vanilla in. Mix reserved oat mixture, salt, baking soda and flour. Put into creamed mixture slowly. Blend well then mix the chips in.
3. By tablespoonfuls, drop onto baking sheets without grease, 2 inches apart. Bake until it turns light brown or for 11 to 13 minutes at 350 degrees. Allow it to cool then let to cool completely by transferring into wire racks.
4. Mix the icing ingredients until it becomes smooth then drizzle on top of cookies. Leave until set and keep in an airtight container.

Nutrition Information: Calories: 124 calories Total Carbohydrate: 17 g Cholesterol: 17 mg Total Fat: 6 g Fiber: 0 g Protein: 1 g Sodium: 84 mg

Spiced Brownie Bites

Serving: about 3-1/2 dozen. | Prep: 40m | Ready in: 55m

Ingredients

- 8 oz. bittersweet chocolate, coarsely chopped
- 1/2 cup butter, cubed
- 4 large eggs
- 1 cup sugar
- 3/4 cup packed brown sugar
- 1-1/4 cups all-purpose flour
- 1/3 cup baking cocoa
- 3/4 tsp. cayenne pepper
- 3/4 tsp. Chinese five-spice powder
- 1/2 tsp. salt
- GLAZE:
- 1 cup (6 oz.) semisweet chocolate chips

- 4 tbsps. butter, cubed
- 1 tbsp. light corn syrup
- Chopped crystallized ginger

Direction

1. Heat the oven beforehand to 350 degrees. Melt butter and chocolate on top of double boiler or in a metal bowl over barely simmering water. Stir until smooth. Allow to cool slightly.
2. Stir sugars and eggs until combined in a big bowl. Mix in chocolate mixture. Combine salt, spices, cocoa and flour in a different bowl, then put in the chocolate mixture gradually. Stir well.
3. Put the mixture in to fill nearly full the mini muffin cups with grease. Bake for 12 to 15 minutes until the middle are set; avoid overbaking. Allow to cool for 5 minutes in pans. Let to cool completely by putting on wire racks.
4. Melt butter and chocolate chips with corn syrup while stirring until smooth in the top of a double boiler or in a small metal bowl over barely simmering water. Take off heat. Allow to cool for about 30 minutes until slightly thickened.
5. Dunk the tops of the brownies in the glaze; put ginger on top.

Nutrition Information: Calories: 137 calories Total Carbohydrate: 16 g Cholesterol: 26 mg Total Fat: 7 g Fiber: 1 g Protein: 2 g Sodium: 63 mg

Stained Glass Heart Cutout Cookies

Serving: about 1-1/2 dozen. | Prep: 15m | Ready in: 25m

Ingredients

- 1/2 cup butter, softened
- 3/4 cup sugar
- 2 eggs
- 1 tsp. vanilla extract
- 2-1/3 cups all-purpose flour
- 1 tsp. baking powder
- 1/3 cup crushed clear red hard candy
- 1 cup vanilla frosting, optional
- 4 drops red food coloring, optional

Direction

1. Cream sugar and butter in bowl; one by one, add eggs, beating well with every addition. Beat vanilla in. Mix baking powder and flour; add to creamed mixture slowly. Cover; refrigerate till easy to handle, about 3 hours.
2. Roll dough out to 1/8-in. thick on lightly floured surface. Use 4-in. heart-shaped cookie cutter that is dipped in flour to cut; cut centers out with 1 1/4-in. heart-shaped cookie cutter. Put aside to reroll. Put cookies on foil-lined baking sheets that are lightly greased, 1-in. apart. Use crushed candy to fill middles.
3. Bake for 7-9 minutes till cookies' edges start to brown and candy melts at 375°. On baking sheets, cool completely. Peel cookies off foil carefully. If desired, mix food coloring and frosting; pipe around edges.

Nutrition Information: Calories: 151 calories Total Carbohydrate: 22 g Cholesterol: 37 mg Total Fat: 6 g Fiber: 0 g Protein: 2 g Sodium: 81 mg

Strawberry Pillows

Serving: 5 dozen. | Prep: 30m | Ready in: 40m

Ingredients

- 1 cup butter, softened
- 1 package (8 oz.) cream cheese, softened
- 1 cup sugar
- 1-1/2 tsps. vanilla extract
- 2-3/4 cups all-purpose flour
- 2/3 cup strawberry preserves

Direction

1. Cream sugar, cream cheese and butter till fluffy and light; beat vanilla in. Beat flour in slowly; divide dough to 4 portions. Form each into a disk; use plastic to wrap. Refrigerate for 2 hours till firm enough to roll.
2. Preheat an oven to 375°; roll each dough portion to 1/8-in. thick on floured surface. Use floured 2-in. round cookie cutter to cut; put 1/2 of the circles on ungreased baking sheets. Put 1/2 tsp. preserves in middle of every circle; put leftover circles over. Use fork to lightly press edges to seal; cut slits over top of every cookie. Bake for 7-9 minutes till edges lightly brown. Transfer from pans onto wire racks; cool.

Nutrition Information: Calories: 83 calories Total Carbohydrate: 10 g Cholesterol: 12 mg Total Fat: 4 g Fiber: 0 g Protein: 1 g Sodium: 36 mg

Strawberry Shortcake Cookies

Serving: about 1-1/2 dozen. | Prep: 35m | Ready in: 50m

Ingredients

- 2 cups all-purpose flour
- 1/2 cup granulated sugar
- Dash salt
- 2/3 cup cold butter
- 2 tbsps. water
- 1 tsp. vanilla extract
- FROSTING:
- 1/4 cup butter, softened
- Scant 1/2 cup sliced fresh strawberries
- 1 tbsp. 2% milk
- 2-1/2 cups confectioners' sugar
- Additional sliced fresh strawberries, optional

Direction

1. Whisk salt, sugar and flour; cut butter in till it looks like coarse crumbs. Mix vanilla and water; mix into crumb mixture till just moist. Refrigerate for 1-2 hours, covered, till firm.
2. Preheat an oven to 325°. Roll out dough to 1/4-inch thick on a lightly floured surface. Use 3-inch floured round cookie cutter to cut. Put on greased baking sheets, 1-inch apart. Bake for 15-18 minutes till lightly browned. Cool for 2 minutes; transfer to wire racks. Completely cool.
3. Frosting: Beat milk, strawberries and butter till combined. Add confectioners' sugar slowly. Beat till blended. Spread on cookies; top with extra sliced strawberries if desired.

Nutrition Information: Calories: 223 calories Total Carbohydrate: 33 g Cholesterol: 25 mg Total Fat: 10 g Fiber: 0 g Protein: 2 g Sodium: 157 mg

Strawberry Valentine Cookies

Serving: about 2 dozen. | Prep: 50m | Ready in: 60m

Ingredients

• 2/3 cup butter, softened
• 2/3 cup sugar
• 1 egg
• 1 tbsp. lemon juice
• 2 cups all-purpose flour
• 1/3 cup strawberry drink mix
• 2 tsps. baking powder
• 1/2 tsp. salt
• GLAZE:
• 1 cup (6 oz.) semisweet chocolate chips
• 1 tsp. shortening
• FROSTING:
• 1/3 cup butter, softened
• 2 tbsps. strawberry drink mix
• 1/8 tsp. salt
• 3 cups confectioners' sugar
• 3 to 5 tbsps. 2% milk

Direction

1. Preheat an oven to 350°. Cream sugar and butter till fluffy and light in small bowl; beat lemon juice and egg in. Mix salt, baking powder, drink mix and flour; add to creamed mixture slowly. Stir well.
2. Roll dough out to 1/4-in. thick on lightly floured surface. Use floured 2 1/2-3-in. heart-shaped cookie cutter to cut; put on ungreased baking sheets, 2-in. apart. Bake till set and edges start to brown, about 8-10 minutes. Cool for 2 minutes. Transfer onto wire racks; completely cool.
3. Melt shortening and chocolate chips in microwave; mix till smooth. Spread on cookies; stand till set.
4. Beat salt, drink mix and butter till blended in small bowl; beat confectioners' sugar in slowly. Add enough milk to get preferred consistency; decorate cookies.

Nutrition Information: Calories: 231 calories Total Carbohydrate: 35 g Cholesterol: 28 mg Total Fat: 10 g Fiber: 1 g Protein: 2 g Sodium: 178 mg

Striped Icebox Cookies

Serving: 5 dozen. | Prep: 30m | Ready in: 40m

Ingredients

- 1 cup butter, softened
- 1-1/2 cups sugar
- 1 large egg
- 2-1/2 cups all-purpose flour
- 1-1/2 tsps. baking powder
- 1/4 tsp. salt
- 1/4 cup chopped maraschino cherries, drained
- 2 drops red food coloring
- 2 oz. semisweet chocolate, melted
- 4 tsps. nonpareils

Direction

1. Cream sugar and butter till fluffy and light; beat egg in. Whisk salt, baking powder and flour in a different bowl; beat into creamed mixture slowly.
2. Divide into thirds; add food coloring and cherries to one portion, chocolate to the second portion then nonpareils to leftover portion.
3. Line waxed paper on 9x5-in. loaf pan; spread cherry dough on bottom. Use chocolate dough to cover then leftover dough; refrigerate for 2 hours till firm, covered.
4. Preheat an oven to 375°; take dough out of pan. Lengthwise, cut in half; cut every portion to 1/4-in. slices. Freeze for 10-15 minutes till firm to easily handle. Bake on lightly greased baking sheets, 1-in. apart, for 10-12 minutes till edges start to brown. Transfer onto wire racks; cool.

Nutrition Information: Calories: 74 calories Total Carbohydrate: 10 g Cholesterol: 11 mg Total Fat: 4 g Fiber: 0 g Protein: 1 g Sodium: 46 mg

Sugarless Heart Cookies

Serving: about 3 dozen. | Prep: 15m | Ready in: 25m

Ingredients

- 3/4 cup butter, softened
- 1 package (.3 oz.) sugar-free raspberry gelatin
- 1/4 cup egg substitute
- 1 tsp. vanilla extract
- 1-3/4 cups all-purpose flour
- 1/2 tsp. baking powder

Direction

1. Cream the gelatin and butter until fluffy and light in a small bowl. Beat in vanilla and egg substitute. Whisk baking powder and flour in a different bowl then beat into the creamed mixture gradually. Make a disk shape out of the dough then wrap with plastic. Put it in the refrigerator until firm enough to roll or for an hour.
2. Heat the oven beforehand to 400 degrees. Roll the dough to 1/4 inch thickness on a lightly floured surface. Cut it using a 1-3/4 inch floured heart-shaped cookie cutter ; put on baking sheets without grease, leaving 1 inch space apart. Bake until bottoms are light brown and set or for 6 to 8 minutes. Allow it to cool by transfer to wire racks from pans.

Nutrition Information: Calories: 59 calories Total Carbohydrate: 5 g Cholesterol: 0 mg Total Fat: 4 g Fiber: 0 g Protein: 1 g Sodium: 49 mg

Sweetheart Coconut Cookies

Serving: about 3-1/2 dozen. | Prep: 30m | Ready in: 40m

Ingredients

- 1 cup sweetened shredded coconut
- 1 cup sugar
- 3/4 cup cold butter, cubed
- 2-1/4 cups all-purpose flour
- 2 large eggs, lightly beaten
- 1/2 tsp. vanilla extract
- GLAZE:
- 3/4 cup confectioners' sugar
- 1 tbsp. water
- 1/2 tsp. vanilla extract
- Coarse white sugar, optional
- 1/2 cup seedless raspberry jam

Direction

1. In a food processor, put sugar and coconut. Put the cover and process the coconut until it is chopped coarsely. Slice butter into the flour in a big bowl until it becomes crumbly. Mix the coconut mixture in, then mix in the vanilla and eggs.
2. Make 1/8 inch thickness dough by rolling it out on a lightly floured surface. Use a 2 1/2 inches heart-shaped cookie cutter that is dipped in the flour. Cut out the middle of half of the cookies using a 1-inch heart-shaped cookie cutter. If desired, roll the small cutouts again.
3. Put the solid and cutout cookies on baking sheets with grease, 1 inch apart. Bake it until edges become lightly browned or for 7 to 9mins at 375 degrees.
4. Mix the vanilla, water and confectioners' sugar in a small bowl. Use the cutout centers to brush over warm cookies. If desired, sprinkle using coarse white sugar immediately. Over the bottom of each solid cookie, spread half tsp. of jam. On top of jam, put cookies with cutout centers.

Nutrition Information: Calories: 104 calories Total Carbohydrate: 16 g Cholesterol: 19 mg Total Fat: 4 g

Fiber: 0 g Protein: 1 g Sodium: 42 mg

Sweetheart Slices

Serving: about 2 dozen. | Prep: 20m | Ready in: 35m

Ingredients

- 1 cup butter, softened
- 3/4 cup sugar
- 4 large egg yolks
- 3 tsps. vanilla extract
- 2-1/2 cups all-purpose flour
- 1-1/2 tsps. ground cinnamon
- 1/3 cup miniature semisweet chocolate chips
- Red or pink paste food coloring

Direction

1. Cream sugar and butter till fluffy and light; one by one, add egg yolks, beating well with every addition. Beat vanilla in. Whisk cinnamon and flour; add to creamed mixture slowly. Stir well. Divide dough to 2 portions; 1/3 of dough and 2/ Mix chocolate chips into bigger portion; put aside. Tint leftover dough pink.
2. Roll smaller portion to 1/2-in. thick on lightly floured surface. Use 1-in. heart-shaped cookie cutter to cut; brush water on one side of hearts; stack together gently to make two 5-in. long logs. Along sides, run finger to smooth edges. Refrigerate till firm, 30 minutes.
3. Divide the chocolate chip dough to 10 portions then roll each to 5-in. coil. Brush water on the outside of heart log; around heart logs, mold coils, pressing gently to adhere. Tightly wrap cookie logs in plastic; mold dough by rolling into smooth roll. Freeze till firm, 2 hours.
4. Preheat an oven to 350°; cut to 1/4-in. slices. Put on parchment paper-lined baking sheets, 2-in. apart. Bake for 12-14 minutes till edges lightly brown; cool for 2 minutes on pans. Transfer to wire racks; cool.

Tender Sugar Cookies

Serving: 5-1/2 dozen. | Prep: 30m | Ready in: 40m

Ingredients

- 3/4 cup butter-flavored shortening
- 1-1/2 cups sugar
- 2 eggs
- 1/2 tsp. almond extract
- 1/2 tsp. vanilla extract
- 3 cups all-purpose flour
- 1 tsp. baking powder
- 1 tsp. baking soda

- 1/2 tsp. salt
- 1/3 cup buttermilk
- Colored sugar and/or coarse sugar

Direction

1. Cream the sugar and shortening until fluffy and light in a big bowl. Put eggs, 1 at a time. Stir well before putting the next. Stir in extracts. Mix salt, baking soda, baking powder and flour then put in the creamed mixture with the buttermilk alternately. Stir well before putting the next. Cover and put in the refrigerator for a minimum of 2 hours.
2. Make 1-inch balls by rolling. Dunk the tops in the sugar. Put on baking sheets lined with parchment paper, leaving 2-inch space apart. Bake until the tops crack and lightly browned or for 9 to 11 minutes at 375 degrees. Allow to cool by putting on wire racks.

Nutrition Information: Calories: 61 calories Total Carbohydrate: 9 g Cholesterol: 6 mg Total Fat: 2 g Fiber: 0 g Protein: 1 g Sodium: 47 mg

Tiny Tim Sandwich Cookies

Serving: about 5 dozen. | Prep: 45m | Ready in: 55m

Ingredients

- 1 cup granulated sugar, divided
- 2 to 3 drops red food coloring
- 2 to 3 drops green food coloring
- 1/2 cup butter, softened
- 1/2 cup shortening
- 1/4 cup confectioners' sugar
- 1 tsp. almond extract
- 2-1/3 cups all-purpose flour
- FROSTING:
- 2 cups confectioners' sugar
- 3 tbsps. butter, softened
- 4-1/2 tsps. heavy whipping cream
- 3/4 tsp. almond extract
- Red and green food coloring, optional

Direction

1. Heat the oven beforehand to 375 degrees. Mix red food coloring and half cup of sugar then leave aside. Mix remaining sugar with green food coloring in a different bowl; reserve.
2. Cream the confectioners' sugar, shortening and butter until fluffy and light in a big bowl. Stir in extract then stir the flour in gradually. Form to 1/2-inch balls.
3. Put on baking sheets without grease, leaving 1-inch space apart. Use cooking spray to coat the bottoms of two glasses. Dip one glass in green sugar and other glass in red sugar. Flatten the cookies using prepped glasses alternatively, dipping them again in sugar as needed. Bake for 8 to 10 minutes until

edges turn light brown. Allow to cool completely by putting on wire racks.

4. Mix extract, cream, butter and confectioners' sugar for the frosting. Use green food coloring to tint half of the frosting and use red food coloring to tint the other half. Frost the bottoms of half of the cookies then cover using the leftover cookies.

Nutrition Information: Calories: 83 calories Total Carbohydrate: 12 g Cholesterol: 6 mg Total Fat: 4 g Fiber: 0 g Protein: 1 g Sodium: 17 mg

Triple Chocolate Kisses

Serving: *3-1/2 dozen. | Prep: 30m | Ready in: 45m*

Ingredients

- 2 egg whites
- 1/4 tsp. cream of tartar
- 1/4 tsp. almond extract
- 1/2 cup sugar
- 1 oz. semisweet chocolate, grated
- 42 milk chocolate kisses
- Baking cocoa

Direction

1. Put egg whites in a bowl then allow to rest for 30 minutes at room temperature.
2. Put extract and cream of tartar. Beat until get soft peaks formed on medium speed. Put the sugar in gradually, a tbsp. at a time while mixing on high until sugar is dissolved and get stiff glossy peaks formed. Fold the grated chocolate in.
3. In a plastic or pastry bag, insert medium open-star tip. Put meringue in to fill the bag. Pipe 42 circles that are 1-inch in size on lightly greased baking sheets.
4. Press a chocolate kiss in the middle of each circle. Pipe the meringue around each chocolate kiss until it is completely covered in continuous rounds from the bottom to the top. Dust using cocoa.
5. Bake until the edges turn light brown or for 15 to 18 minutes at 325 degrees. Allow to cool by immediately putting on wire racks; keep in an airtight container.

Nutrition Information: Calories: 76 calories Total Carbohydrate: 11 g Cholesterol: 2 mg Total Fat: 3 g Fiber: 0 g Protein: 1 g Sodium: 13 mg

Triple Nut Snowballs

Serving: *about 6 dozen. | Prep: 15m | Ready in: 25m*

Ingredients

- 1 cup plus 2 tbsps. unsalted butter, softened
- 1/2 cup plus 2 cups confectioners' sugar, divided
- 1-1/2 tsps. almond extract
- 2 cups all-purpose flour

- 1 tsp. salt
- 1 tsp. ground cinnamon
- 1 cup unsalted cashews
- 1 cup macadamia nuts
- 1 cup pecan halves

Direction

1. Preheat an oven to 375°. Cream 1/2 cup confectioners' sugar and butter till fluffy and light; beat extract in. Whisk cinnamon, salt and flour in separate bowl; beat into creamed mixture slowly. Pulse nuts till finely ground in food processor; mix nuts into dough.
2. Form to 1-in. balls; put on parchment paper-lined baking sheets, 1-in. apart. Bake for 8-10 minutes till golden brown; cool for 10 minutes on pans.
3. Put leftover confectioners' sugar in small bowl; in sugar, roll slightly cooled cookies. Put cookies on wire racks; completely cool. Before serving, roll cookies again in sugar.

Nutrition Information: Calories: 88 calories Total Carbohydrate: 8 g Cholesterol: 8 mg Total Fat: 6 g Fiber: 0 g Protein: 1 g Sodium: 40 mg

Triple-chocolate Brownie Cookies

Serving: 6 dozen. | Prep: 25m | Ready in: 35m

Ingredients

- 4 oz. unsweetened chocolate, chopped
- 3/4 cup butter, cubed
- 4 eggs
- 2 cups sugar
- 1-1/2 cups all-purpose flour
- 1/2 cup baking cocoa
- 2 tsps. baking powder
- 1/2 tsp. salt
- 2 cups (12 oz.) semisweet chocolate chips, divided
- 2 tsps. shortening

Direction

1. Melt butter and chocolate in microwave; mix till smooth. Slightly cool. Beat sugar and eggs in big bowl; mix chocolate mixture in. Mix salt, baking powder, cocoa and flour; add to chocolate mixture slowly. Stir well; mix 1 1/2 cups chocolate chips in. Cover; refrigerate till easy to handle, 2 hours.
2. Preheat an oven to 350°; drop by tablespoonfuls on greased baking sheets, 2-in. apart. Bake till tops slightly crack and edges set, about 7-9 minutes. Cool for 2 minutes; transfer from pans onto wire racks. Completely cool.
3. Melt shortening and leftover chips in microwave; mix till smooth then drizzle on cookies. Stand till chocolate is set, about 30 minutes; keep in airtight container.

Nutrition Information: Calories: 79 calories Total Carbohydrate: 11 g Cholesterol: 17 mg Total Fat: 4 g

Fiber: 1 g Protein: 1 g Sodium: 51 mg

Valentine Butter Cookies

Serving: 18-19 dozen. | Prep: 30m | Ready in: 40m

Ingredients

• 2 cups butter, softened
• 2 cups sugar
• 3 eggs
• 1 tbsp. vanilla extract
• 6 cups all-purpose flour
• 2 tsps. baking powder
• Red colored sugar, optional

Direction

1. Cream the sugar and butter in a bowl. Put vanilla and eggs. Stir well. Combine baking powder and flour. Put in the creamed mixture gradually and stir well.
2. Use a cookie press to shape the cookies. Put on baking sheets without grease. If desired, decorate them using sugar. Bake until edges turn light brown or for 10 to 12 minutes at 350 degrees.

Nutrition Information: Calories: 68 calories Total Carbohydrate: 9 g Cholesterol: 14 mg Total Fat: 3 g Fiber: 0 g Protein: 1 g Sodium: 41 mg

Valentine Cookie Bouquet

Serving: 2 dozen. | Prep: 25m | Ready in: 45m

Ingredients

• 1 cup butter, softened
• 1 cup sugar
• 1/4 cup milk
• 1 egg
• 1 tsp. vanilla extract
• 2-3/4 cups all-purpose flour
• 1/2 cup baking cocoa
• 3/4 tsp. baking powder
• 1/4 tsp. baking soda
• 24 long wooden skewers
• FROSTING:
• 1/2 cup butter, softened
• 2 cups confectioners' sugar
• 2 to 3 tbsps. maraschino cherry juice

Direction

1. Cream sugar and butter till fluffy and light in big bowl; beat vanilla, egg and milk in. Mix baking soda, baking powder, cocoa and flour; add to creamed mixture. Stir well. Cover; refrigerate till easy to handle, 1 hour.
2. Roll 1/2 dough out to 1/8-in. thick on lightly floured surface; use floured 3-in. heart-shaped cookie cutter to cut out. Put on ungreased baking sheets, 1-in. apart.
3. With 1 end of each skewer 1-in. from top of every heart, put skewers over each cookie. Press into dough gently; put a little additional dough on top of each skewer then press into cookie to make it secure.
4. Bake for 8-10 minutes till firm at 350°; stand for 2 minutes. Transfer to wire racks; cool.
5. Roll leftover dough out on lightly floured surface; use floured 3-in. heart-shaped cookie cutter to cut out. Use 1-in. heart-shaped cookie cutter to cut centers out.
6. Bake for 8-10 minutes at 350° till firm; stand for 2 minutes. Transfer to wire racks; cool.
7. Mix confectioners' sugar, butter and enough cherry juice to get spreading consistency in small bowl; spread frosting on cookies with skewers gently. Put cutout centers over cookies.

Nutrition Information: Calories: 234 calories Total Carbohydrate: 31 g Cholesterol: 40 mg Total Fat: 12 g Fiber: 1 g Protein: 2 g Sodium: 146 mg

Valentine Cookies

Serving: 3 dozen. | Prep: 20m | Ready in: 35m

Ingredients

- 1 cup butter, softened
- 1 cup sugar
- 1 egg
- 3 tsps. vanilla extract
- 2 tsps. almond extract
- 2-1/2 cups all-purpose flour
- 1 tsp. baking powder
- 1/4 tsp. salt
- Prepared vanilla frosting and red colored sugar, optional

Direction

1. Cream the sugar and butter in a big bowl. Put the egg and stir well. Put the extracts; beat well. Mix salt, baking powder and flour, then put into the creamed mixture until blended. Cover and put in the refrigerator until easy to handle or for 3 hours.
2. Make 1/8-inch thickness dough by rolling out on a lightly floured surface. Slice using a 3-inch heart shaped cookie cutter that was immersed in flour. Put on baking sheets without grease, leaving 1-inch space apart.
3. Bake until lightly browned or for 13 to 15 minutes at 325 degrees. Allow to cool by putting on wire racks. If desired, decorate using colored sugar and frosting.

Nutrition Information: Calories: 204 calories Total Carbohydrate: 24 g Cholesterol: 39 mg Total Fat: 11 g Fiber: 0 g Protein: 2 g Sodium: 162 mg

Valentine Sugar Cookies

Serving: 3-1/2 dozen. | Prep: 10m | Ready in: 20m

Ingredients

- 1 cup butter, softened
- 1-1/2 cups confectioners' sugar
- 1 egg, lightly beaten
- 1 tsp. vanilla extract
- 1 tsp. almond extract
- 2-1/2 cups all-purpose flour
- Red decorator's sugar, optional

Direction

1. Cream the sugar and butter in a bowl. Put extracts and egg; mix in flour. Stir well then put in the refrigerator for several hours. Make 1/4-inch thickness dough by rolling on lightly floured surface. Slice the dough using a 2 1/2 or 3-inch heart-shaped cookie cutter then put on baking sheets without grease. If desired, sprinkle sugar. Bake until lightly browned or for 8 to 10 minutes at 375 degrees.

Nutrition Information: Calories: 169 calories Total Carbohydrate: 20 g Cholesterol: 33 mg Total Fat: 9 g Fiber: 0 g Protein: 2 g Sodium: 91 mg

Walnut Chocolate Hearts

Serving: about 4 dozen. | Prep: 30m | Ready in: 40m

Ingredients

- 1 cup butter, cubed
- 2/3 cup packed brown sugar
- 1 tsp. vanilla extract
- 1 egg, lightly beaten
- 2-1/4 cups all-purpose flour
- 1/4 cup baking cocoa
- 1/2 tsp. salt
- 3/4 cup finely chopped walnuts
- TOPPING:
- 1-1/2 cups semisweet chocolate chips
- 2 tbsps. shortening

- 1/2 cup ground walnuts

Direction

1. Mix and cook brown sugar and butter in big saucepan on medium-low heat till butter melts; take off hea

Mix vanilla in. Cool for 15 minutes; mix egg in.

2. Mix salt, cocoa and flour; add to butter mixture. Fold walnuts in. Cover; refrigerate till easy to handle, about 30 minutes.
3. Preheat an oven to 350°. Roll dough to 1/4-in. thick on lightly floured surface. Use floured 3-in. heart-shaped cookie cutter to cut; put on ungreased baking sheets, 1-in. apart.
4. Bake till edges are firm, about 9-10 minutes. Put on wire racks to cool.
5. Topping: Melt shortening and chocolate chips in microwave; mix till smooth. Dip 1/2 of every heart to chocolate mixture; let excess drip off. Dip dipped side's edges in ground walnuts. Put on waxed paper; stand till set.

Nutrition Information: Calories: 233 calories Total Carbohydrate: 23 g Cholesterol: 29 mg Total Fat: 15 g Fiber: 1 g Protein: 3 g Sodium: 133 mg

White Chocolate Raspberry Cookies

Serving: about 3-1/2 dozen. | Prep: 25m | Ready in: 35m

Ingredients

- 1 cup butter, softened
- 2/3 cup sugar
- 4 oz. white baking chocolate, melted
- 1 egg
- 2 tsps. vanilla extract
- 2-1/4 cups all-purpose flour
- 1 tsp. baking powder
- 1/4 tsp. salt
- TOPPING:
- 1 jar (12 oz.) seedless raspberry jam
- 4 oz. white baking chocolate, melted

Direction

1. Cream the sugar and butter until fluffy and light in a big bowl. Stir in vanilla, egg and chocolate. Mix salt, baking powder and flour, then put in the creamed mixture gradually. Stir well.
2. Form to 1-inch balls; put them on baking sheets without grease, leaving 1-inch space apart. Create an indentation in the middle of each cookie using a wooden spoon handle. Bake until set or for 9 to 11 minutes at 375 degrees.
3. Allow to cool completely by putting on wire racks. Into cookies, spoon the jam. Use chocolate to sprinkle over. Allow to rest until set then keep in an airtight container.

Nutrition Information: Calories: 128 calories Total Carbohydrate: 17 g Cholesterol: 18 mg Total Fat: 6 g Fiber: 0 g Protein: 1 g Sodium: 62 mg

White Chocolate Raspberry Thumbprints

Serving: about 3 dozen. | Prep: 25m | Ready in: 35m

Ingredients

- 3/4 cup butter, softened
- 1/2 cup packed brown sugar
- 2 eggs, separated
- 1-1/4 cups all-purpose flour
- 1/4 cup baking cocoa
- 1-1/4 cups finely chopped pecans or walnuts
- FILLING:
- 4 oz. white baking chocolate, coarsely chopped
- 2 tbsps. butter
- 1/4 cup seedless raspberry jam

Direction

1. Cream brown sugar and butter till fluffy and light in big bowl; beat egg yolks in. Mix cocoa and flour; add to creamed mixture slowly. Stir well. Cover; refrigerate till easy to handle for 1-2 hours.
2. Whisk egg whites till foamy in shallow bowl; put nuts in separate shallow bowl. Form dough to 1-in. balls then dip in egg whites; roll in nuts.
3. Make an indentation in middle of each cookie with wooden spoon handle; put on greased baking sheets, 1-in. apart. Bake for 8-10 minutes till set at 350°. Transfer to wire racks; cool.
4. Melt butter and white chocolate in microwave; mix till smooth. Put 1/2 tsp. in each cookie. Put 1/4 tsp. jam on each; keep in airtight container.

Yummy Cracker Snacks

Serving: 4 dozen. | Prep: 60m | Ready in: 60m

Ingredients

- 96 Ritz crackers
- 1 cup creamy peanut butter
- 1 cup marshmallow creme
- 2 lbs. milk chocolate candy coating, melted
- Holiday sprinkles, optional

Direction

1. Use peanut butter to spread half of the crackers. Use marshmallow crème to spread remaining crackers. Form a sandwich by putting the crème side down on top of the peanut butter crackers.
2. Immerse the sandwiches in the melted candy coating. Let the excess coating to drip off. Put on pans lined with wax papers then place in the refrigerator until set or for 15 minutes. Drizzle using more candy coating and use sprinkles to decorate if desired. Keep in airtight container.

Nutrition Information: Calories: 170 calories Total Carbohydrate: 19 g Cholesterol: 0 mg Total Fat: 10 g Fiber: 1 g Protein: 2 g Sodium: 89 mg

Printed in Great Britain
by Amazon